RECIPES 4 LIFE
Fighting Back with Food

Created in collaboration with
The Alfie Gough Trust
Registered Charity Number 1144380

This book is dedicated in memory of

Alfie Gough

11/04/2008 – 29/07/2010

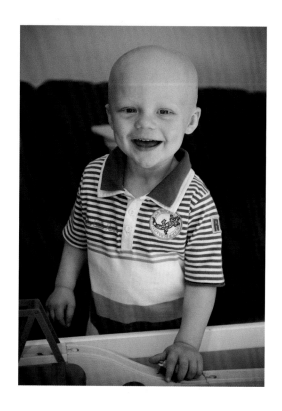

Our beautiful baby boy.

Alfie we had to let you go, we know that you are now safe.
The emptiness & sadness is so hard for us to bear.
There has been so many times that we wanted just to
pick you up & hold you close.
We will never stop feeling the love you have left behind.

A million times we will miss you a million times we will cry,
If love alone could have saved you,
you never would have died.

Mummy & Daddy x x

Alfie's full story can be read at: **www.alfiestrust.com**

RECIPES 4 LIFE

Fighting Back with Food

Created in collaboration with
The Alfie Gough Trust
Regestered Charity Number 1144380

All proceeds from the sale of this book goes directly to the **Alfie Gough Trust** (Registered Charity).

ecademyPRESS
www.ecademy-press.com

Recipes 4 Life
Fighting Back With Food

First published in 2012 by

Ecademy Press
48 St Vincent Drive, St Albans, Hertfordshire, AL1 5SJ
info@ecademy-press.com
www.ecademy-press.com

Printed and bound by Pratiroop Mudran, India

Designed by Arlene Danton and Michael Inns
Typesetting by Karen Gladwell

Printed on acid-free paper from managed forests. This book is
printed on demand, so no copies will be remaindered or pulped.

ISBN 978-1-907722-96-7

Contents

FISH

CHICKEN DISHES

RECIPES 4LIFE

Nothing prepares you for the news that your child has cancer.
We never stopped fighting & with so many support networks
& methods available, we learnt how to integrate with the treatment;
one key element being correct nutrition to help combat the severe
treatment side effects. Alfie had quality of life, we refused to let
anything get in the way of this & we have so many happy memories.
This is why we have chosen to fund nutritional therapy involvement.
We learnt that Nutrition is the fundamental foundation.

A fund for Alfie was set up to pay for treatment outside of the UK.

Sadly Alfie died before this was possible. We decided to keep
raising money & all funds raised will be used to help others;
& this book is where it all begins.

Fighting Back with Food

www.alfiestrust.com

Information on Ingredients
Found in Our Recipes

Throughout our book we refer to the use of 'organic' food ingredients. The reason for this is because organic foods are not sprayed with chemical fertilisers & pesticides or genetically modified organisms.

Organic foods are not processed using iridation, solvents & chemical food additives - unlike non-organic foods. By avoiding the consumption of processed foods, the human body is not taking in the toxins that is contained within non-organic ingredients.

We encourage water purification to remove undesirable chemicals, materials & biological contaminants from contaminated tap water.

We encourage you to avoid non-stick pans & plastic, replacing them with stainless steel, stone, ceramic & glass.

Our foods are all free of cow's milk dairy, which contains insulin-like growth factor; this is a natural structure within the milk, which has been linked to increased proliferation of cells.

Our recipes are also free of refined sugars; glucose is the choice of fuel for cancer cells.

Foods free of refined sugars are not just important for cancer clients, but for the well being of all adults & children alike.

 Wheat Free
Gluten Free
Dairy Free
Vegetarian

We also include a helpful reference guide for each recipe - to help you create a meal suited to your own dietary requirements.

For more information on:
Organic food, water purification, cow's milk dairy, cooking methods, balancing blood sugars through eating a well balanced diet & creating an anti-cancer environment for the body please visit
www.alfiestrust.com.

We also recommend the following web sites, with regards to recipe ingredients for use with this cook book & further information:

www.bobbyshealthyshop.co.uk
www.buytrehalose.co.uk

How to Soak & Cook Beans

We refer to using soaked beans in a number of our recipes, therefore we have provided you with a guide which shows you how:

INGREDIENTS
Serves 2

1 cup dried beans

METHOD

Pick out any dried, withered or discoloured beans.

Rinse under filtered water.

Place beans in a container with a lid & pour 3 cups of filtered water over beans.

Soak for 6 hours *(if soaked for too long, they may ferment, which affects their flavour & may make them difficult to digest)*.

Drain & rinse.

After soaking, drain the beans & add fresh water to the cooking pot.

Bring the beans to the boil, lower heat & simmer for 60-90 minutes or until beans are tender *(check packaging as beans vary)*.

If needed, add more filtered water to the simmering pot.

Beans are cooked when they can be mashed with a fork.

Soaking beans allows the dried beans to absorb the water, which begins to dissolve the starches that cause intestinal discomfort.

STOCKS & SAUCES

RECIPES 4 LIFE

Fighting Back with Food

Apple Chutney

INGREDIENTS
Makes about 7 jars

1.8kg eating apples
(peeled, cored & finely chopped)

570ml un-pasteurized apple cider vinegar

1 clove garlic, crushed

1 large onion, finely chopped

225g rapadura sugar

2 tbsp blackstrap molasses

55g ginger, grated

½ tsp pink Himalayan rock salt

1 tsp pickling spice
(tied in a piece of muslin)

½ tsp cayenne pepper

2–4 tbsp raisins *(optional)*

2–4 fresh chillies or ¼-½ tsp chilli powder *(optional)*

METHOD

Gently sauté the finely chopped onion over a low heat, until transparent. Add the crushed garlic & chillies. Stir for 2 minutes.

Add the apples & half of the vinegar & cook gently for 10–15 minutes.

Add the raisins *(optional),* sugar, ginger, salt & pickling spice & continue to cook for about 1 hour or until thick.

Remove the spices in the muslin & stir in the rest of the vinegar.

Mash using a potato masher.

Put into jars & cover with lid.

Sterilize clean jars by putting them in a cold oven then turning it on to120°C/250°F/Gas Mark ½ for about 40 minutes. Leave them to cool in the oven.

Wheat Free
Gluten Free
Dairy Free
Vegetarian ⓥ

Bright Red Pepper Sauce

INGREDIENTS

Serves 2

2 garlic cloves *(optional)*

1 medium onion, chopped

3 red peppers, chopped

3 tbsp organic olive oil

2 tsp Himalayan rock salt

2 tsp tomato puree

pinch of paprika

300ml distilled water

METHOD

Soften the vegetables a little in the oil at medium heat.

Add the remaining Ingredients, stirring after each addition & adding the distilled water last.

Reduce the heat, cover & cook gently until the peppers are very soft *(about 30 minutes)*.

Allow to cool a little & mix until smooth in the blender.

Wheat Free
Gluten Free
Dairy Free
V Vegetarian

Cheesy Garlic Mayonnaise

INGREDIENTS
Serves 2

1 tub organic cottage cheese

1 dsp organic mayonnaise

½ tsp honey

½ clove garlic, crushed
(crush 10 minutes before use)

1 tbsp organic flaxseed oil, cold pressed

1 tbsp fresh chives, chopped
(optional)

METHOD

Mix all the ingredients in a bowl with a hand blender until smooth.

Store in the fridge or freeze in portions.

Wheat Free
Gluten Free
Vegetarian V

Coconut Margarine

INGREDIENTS
Makes 1 Jar

250g organic coconut oil
(extra virgin)

1 medium onion, finely chopped

10 cloves garlic
(crushed 10 minutes before use)

125ml organic flaxseed oil,
cold pressed *(refrigerated)*

METHOD

Sauté the onion in the coconut oil over a very low heat, for about 4-5 minutes.
Stir occasionally to prevent sticking.

Add the garlic & continue to sauté gently for 3 minutes.

Allow to cool until the coconut oil just starts to solidify.

Strain the coconut oil through a fine sieve or muslin cloth, into the pre-chilled flaxseed oil.

Pour into a glass jar.

Allow to cool to room temperature.

Store the coconut margarine in the fridge.

Wheat Free
Gluten Free
Dairy Free
V Vegetarian

Creamed Garlic Sauce

INGREDIENTS
Serves 2

1 medium potato, finely chopped
10 garlic cloves, peeled
600ml rice milk or oat milk
pinch dried thyme
pinch ground nutmeg
pinch freshly ground black pepper
1 tsp tamari sauce (optional)

METHOD

Bring everything gently to boil. Cover, reduce the heat & cook very gently for 35 minutes, or until potato & garlic break up when prodded with a fork.

Blend until smooth or push through a mouli or strainer.

Refrigerate, serve when cold.

Wheat Free
Dairy Free
Vegetarian V

7

Garlic Creamed Dressing

INGREDIENTS
Serves 2

100g fresh or silken tofu

2 tasty ripe tomatoes

2 garlic cloves, peeled & chopped

1 small mild onion or shallot, grated

1 tsp tamari sauce

¼ tsp freshly ground black pepper

METHOD

Mix in a blender until smooth.

Chill; serve when cold.

- Wheat Free
- Gluten Free
- Dairy Free
- V Vegetarian

Gluten Free Gravy

INGREDIENTS
Serves 2

1 tbsp cornflour *(cornstarch)*

250ml distilled water, homemade vegetable stock *(see page 16)***, or drained liquid from boiling potatoes or steaming vegetables**

4-6 tbsp juices drained from poultry or meat being roasted

¼ tsp dried mixed herbs

freshly ground black pepper

METHOD

Mix the cornflour with a small quantity *(preferably cold)* from the 250ml of liquid.
This will ensure that the cornflour makes a smooth paste & avoids lumps when the rest of the liquid is added.

Add the rest of the 250ml of liquid to the cornflour paste in a small saucepan, don't add the poultry juices at this stage.

Add the optional herbs, salt & freshly ground black pepper & stir well.

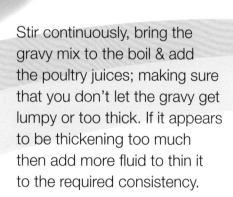

Stir continuously, bring the gravy mix to the boil & add the poultry juices; making sure that you don't let the gravy get lumpy or too thick. If it appears to be thickening too much then add more fluid to thin it to the required consistency.

Leave to simmer over a gentle heat while you prepare meals onto dishes, then decant the gravy into a preheated jug.

Wheat Free
Gluten Free
Dairy Free

Guacamole

INGREDIENTS

Serves 2

2 ripe avocados, peeled & de-stoned

small handful of coriander, chopped

2 garlic cloves, pressed

juice of ½ a lemon

1 small red onion, finely chopped

2 ripe tomatoes, peeled & chopped

a pinch of Himalayan rock salt

a few twists of freshly ground
black pepper

METHOD

Lightly blend all the ingredients together in a food processor.

Serve as a light dip with corn crackers, rice cakes or vegetable sticks.

Wheat Free
Gluten Free
Dairy Free
V Vegetarian

Parsnip Spread

INGREDIENTS
Serves 2

2 parsnips, peeled & chopped

1 carrot, peeled & chopped

2 dsp tahini

1 tsp tamari sauce

METHOD

Cook parsnips & carrot in water until tender.

Put in a food processor & blend together. Add the tahini & tamari sauce then blend for a further 30 seconds.

Put in a dish & cover. Keep refrigerated until required.

Serve by spreading on rice cakes or gluten-free bread.

Wheat Free
Gluten Free
Dairy Free
Vegetarian

Pesto

INGREDIENTS
Serves 2

METHOD

½ clove garlic, crushed

½ tsp pink Himalayan rock salt

110g fresh basil leaves, roughly chopped

55g pine nuts, lightly toasted

80g parmesan cheese, freshly & finely grated

4 tbsp extra virgin olive oil

1 tsp lemon juice *(optional)*

Lightly toast the pine nuts in a dry stainless steel pan over a low to medium heat, shaking the pan frequently to prevent browning/ burning. Allow to cool.

Crush the garlic, salt & basil in a pestle & mortar.

Add the cooled pine nuts & grind together.

Tip the mixture out into a bowl & add the parmesan, olive oil & lemon juice *(optional)*. Mix thoroughly.

Add more olive oil, pine nuts or parmesan according to taste & your preferred texture.

To fully develop the flavours, pesto ideally should be made using a pestle & mortar, but it can also be made using a hand blender or food processor.

Alternatively blend all the ingredients in a food processor or with a hand blender. Adjust the proportions 'to taste' & to your preferred texture.

Wheat Free
Gluten Free
V Vegetarian

Quick Hummus

INGREDIENTS

Serves 4

240g dried chickpeas, soaked & cooked

juice of half a lemon

1 large garlic clove

1 tbsp tahini

75ml extra virgin olive oil

1 tsp Himalayan rock salt *(to taste)*

Keeps up to 5 days in the fridge.

METHOD

Blend all the ingredients together until smooth & creamy. If you want a smoother consistency, add an extra drizzle of olive oil or a splash of water.

Taste & adjust seasoning if required.

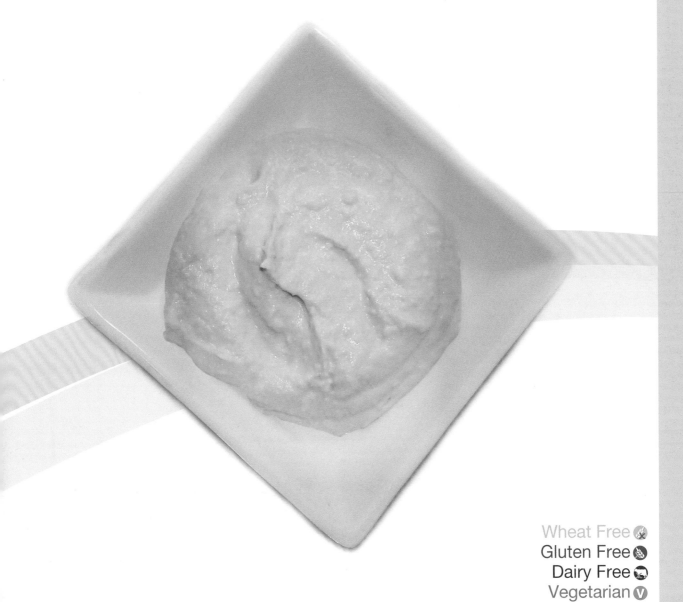

Wheat Free 🌾
Gluten Free 🌾
Dairy Free 🥛
Vegetarian Ⓥ

Tomato Ketchup

INGREDIENTS
Serves 1

4-5 tbsp tomato sauce
(see page 15)

½-1 tsp balsamic vinegar
(good quality organic)

½ tsp maple syrup
(if required)

METHOD

Mix up to taste, adding more or less vinegar, or a little extra maple syrup as desired.

Make up small amounts as needed.

 Wheat Free
 Gluten Free
 Dairy Free
V Vegetarian

Tomato Sauce

INGREDIENTS
Makes approx 1.2ltrs

1 onion, finely chopped

2 cloves garlic
(crushed 10 minutes before use)

1 tbsp extra virgin olive oil

1 bay leaf

6-8 ripe tomatoes, roughly chopped

1 jar organic passata
(strained tomato)

2-4 tsp maple syrup or honey
(sweeten to taste)

good pinch of pink Himalayan rock salt

a few twists of freshly ground black pepper

METHOD

Sauté the onion in the olive oil over a very low heat, for about 20 mins or until soft & lightly caramelised.

Add the crushed garlic, passata, bay leaf & tomatoes.

Add the salt & pepper & slowly bring to the boil.

Leave to simmer gently with the lid off, for about 1hr.

Sweeten to taste.

Remove the bay leaf.

Pass the sauce through a mouli.

Blend with a hand blender to make a smooth sauce.

Once the sauce has cooled, put into jars & freeze.

Wheat Free
Gluten Free
Dairy Free
Vegetarian

Vegetable Stock

INGREDIENTS
Makes 5ltrs

5 carrots, chopped

5 large onions, roughly chopped

8 whole black peppercorns

1 bunch thyme

1 bay leaf

1 leek

freshly-squeezed juice of 1 orange

5ltr water
(distilled or filtered)

METHOD

Put all the chopped vegetables & all the other ingredients in a large stock pan.

Cover with the water.

Bring to the boil & then simmer gently for 4 hours.

Allow to cool.

Strain through a sieve into large containers, discarding the vegetables.

Allow the stock to cool completely before storing in either the fridge or freezer.

SOUPS & STEWS

RECIPES 4 LIFE

Fighting Back with Food

Broccoli & Puy Lentil Soup

INGREDIENTS
Serves 4

110g puy lentils

1 onion, chopped

1 large head of broccoli

1.2ltr water, distilled

1 vegetable stock cube
(gluten free)

METHOD

Add all ingredients to pan, simmer for about 45 minutes.

Blend until smooth.

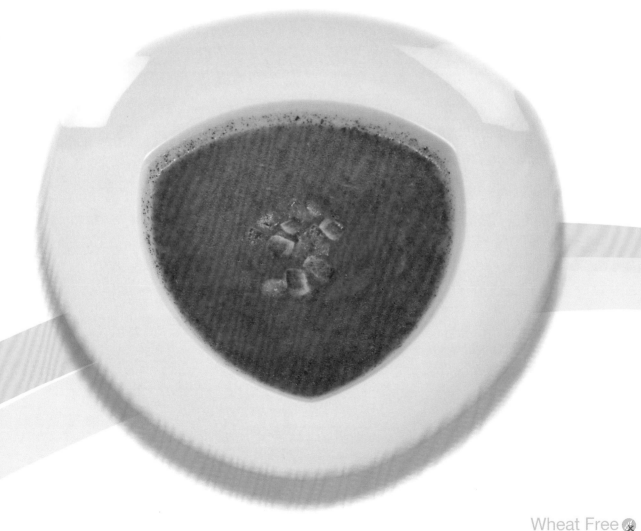

Wheat Free
Gluten Free
Dairy Free
Vegetarian **V**

Carrot & Almond Soup

INGREDIENTS
Serves 4

2 onions, peeled & chopped

2 garlic cloves, peeled & chopped

6 carrots, trimmed, peeled & sliced

1 tbsp wheat-free vegetable bouillon powder

2-3 tbsp chopped fresh coriander, stalks reserved

2-3 tbsp chopped fresh parsley, stalks reserved

100g ground almonds

METHOD

Place the onions, garlic & carrots in a large saucepan. Add 1.25ltr distilled boiling water & the bouillon powder. Bring to the boil & add the herb stalks.

Lower the heat & simmer for 30 minutes until vegetables are tender when pierced with a knife.

Remove from the heat & allow to cool. Strain; reserving the stock. Remove the herb stalks, blend the vegetables in a food processor or with a hand-held blender until smooth.

Return the mixture to the pan & add the ground almonds & enough of the reserved stock to make a soup like consistency.

Reheat, divide between warmed soup bowls & serve garnished with chopped fresh coriander & parsley.

Wheat Free
Gluten Free
Dairy Free
V Vegetarian

Carrot, Coriander & Red Lentil Soup

INGREDIENTS
Serves 4

1kg carrots

110g red lentils

1 onion, chopped

1ltr distilled water

1 vegetable stock cube
(gluten free)

handful of coriander
(fresh)

METHOD

Put all ingredients except coriander in a pan & simmer for 45 minutes.

Add coriander & cook for couple of minutes.

Blend until smooth.

Wheat Free
Gluten Free
Dairy Free
Vegetarian

Curried Aubergine Soup

INGREDIENTS
Serves 4

1 onion, chopped

1 garlic clove, crushed

1 tbsp medium curry powder

1 aubergine, diced

225g carrots, diced

850ml vegetable stock, homemade
(see page 16)

400g jar tomato passata

twist of Himalayan rock salt

1 tbsp chopped fresh coriander
(to garnish)

METHOD

Place the onion, garlic, curry powder, aubergine & carrots in a large saucepan.

Add the stock, chopped tomatoes & seasoning. Bring to the boil & then simmer for 25 minutes, until the aubergine is very pulpy.

Transfer the soup to a food processor or liquidiser in batches. Blend for a very short time, so the texture of the soup in not entirely smooth.

Heat through in a clean saucepan.

Suitable for freezing.

Garnish with coriander.

- Wheat Free
- Gluten Free
- Dairy Free
- V Vegetarian

French Onion Soup

INGREDIENTS
Serves 4

10 medium onions

4 tsp xylitol

1ltr vegetable stock, homemade
(see page 16)

4 garlic cloves

2 tbsp organic olive oil

METHOD

Slice the onions & cook with the xylitol on a low heat in a wok with the garlic & oil until soft.

Prepare the stock & add to the onions. Stir.

Transfer all into Slow Cooker & cook on low for 6-8 hours.

Wheat Free
Gluten Free
Dairy Free
Vegetarian Ⓥ

23

Hemp Pumpkin Soup

INGREDIENTS
Serves 4

METHOD

1 pumpkin or seasonal squash, peeled, deseeded & cut into 2.5cm pieces

1 bunch asparagus, roughly chopped *(tips reserved for a salad)*

2 large sweet potatoes, peeled & cut into 2.5cm pieces

3 carrots, trimmed, peeled & chopped

6 onions, peeled & roughly chopped

1 vegetable stock cube *(gluten free)*

1 garlic clove, peeled & chopped

2 tbsp chopped fresh coriander

2 tbsp shelled hemp seeds

2 tbsp pumpkin seeds

Bring a large pan with 1ltr of distilled water to the boil then add the pumpkin or squash, asparagus, sweet potatoes, carrots, onions & stock cube. Bring back to the boil then lower the heat & simmer for 10-15 minutes or until the vegetables are tender when pierced with a knife.

Remove from the heat & add the garlic & coriander.

Allow to cool then blend in a food processor or with a hand-held blender to your desired consistency.

Reheat gently. Divide between warmed bowls & serve garnished with seeds.

Wheat Free
Gluten Free
Dairy Free
V Vegetarian

Leek & Potato Soup

INGREDIENTS
Serves 8

3 leeks, washed & finely chopped *(most of the green removed)*

25g goat's butter *(or 1 tbsp extra virgin olive oil)*

1 medium onion, finely chopped

1 large potato, peeled & chopped into 2.5cm cubes

a generous pinch of ground pink Himalayan rock salt *(to taste)*

a few twists of freshly ground black pepper

285ml goat's milk

1 ltr vegetable stock *(see page 16)*

METHOD

Wash the leeks thoroughly, removing all traces of soil,

Chop off & discard most of the green part of the leeks & finely slice.

Sauté the onions & the leeks in the goat's butter *(or the olive oil)*, over a very low heat for about 20 minutes, until soft & lightly caramelised. Stir occasionally to prevent sticking.

Add the chopped potato & continue to sauté for 3 or 4 minutes, stirring occasionally.

Add the salt, pepper, stock & goat's milk.

Bring to the boil & simmer for 10 minutes.

Blend to desired consistency using a hand blender or food processor.

Recipe kindly donated by celebrity chef, Gary Rhodes OBE

Wheat Free
Gluten Free
Vegetarian V

Mixed Bean Stew

INGREDIENTS
Serves 4

1 onion, chopped

1 tbsp extra virgin olive oil

1 handful of mushrooms, chopped

1 garlic clove, crushed

1 jar of passata

1 courgette, sliced

400g mixed beans soaked & cooked

a handful of flat
leaf parsley, chopped

METHOD

In a saucepan, sauté the onion in the olive oil until transparent.

Add the mushrooms & garlic then cook for a couple of minutes.

Add all of the rest of the ingredients except the parsley & gently simmer for 15 minutes, or until the vegetables are cooked.

Sprinkle with parsley & serve with brown rice & broccoli florets.

✸ Wheat Free
✿ Gluten Free
◐ Dairy Free
Ⓥ Vegetarian

Spinach Soup

INGREDIENTS
Serves 4

1 onion, peeled & finely chopped

1 tsp organic olive oil

500g fresh spinach

1 vegetable stock cube (gluten free)

1 handful parsley stalks

fresh nutmeg to taste

250ml oat milk

1 tbsp pumpkin seeds

1 handful fresh baby spinach leaves

METHOD

Place the onion, olive oil & 1 tablespoon of water in a large pan. Cook over a low to moderate heat for 2-3 minutes until soft.

Add the spinach, 500ml boiling water, the stock cube & parsley stalks & cook for 5-7 minutes. Allow to cool slightly, then blend in a food processor or with a hand-held blender until smooth.

Return to the pan, season with a little nutmeg, stir in the oat milk (or 250ml water or vegetable stock) & reheat gently.

Divide between warmed bowls & serve garnished with the pumpkin seeds & raw baby spinach leaves.

Wheat Free ⊗
Dairy Free 🥛
Vegetarian Ⓥ

Spinach, Watercress & Puy Lentil Soup

INGREDIENTS
Serves 4

110g puy lentils

1 onion, chopped

75g watercress

200g spinach

1.2ltr distilled water

1 vegetable stock cube
(gluten free)

METHOD

Add all ingredients to pan, simmer for about 45 minutes.

Blend until smooth.

- Wheat Free
- Gluten Free
- Dairy Free
- V Vegetarian

Tomato Soup

INGREDIENTS
Serves 4

METHOD

1 medium onion, chopped

1 clove garlic, crushed

25g extra virgin olive oil

8-10 tomatoes, deseeded & chopped

1 large carrot, sliced

1.15ltr vegetable stock, homemade
(see page 16)

140ml goat's milk

1 bay leaf

1 dsp maple syrup

**a generous pinch of pink
Himalayan rock salt**

**a few twists of freshly ground
black pepper**

Sauté the onion in the goat's butter
& the olive oil, over a very low heat,
for about 20–30 minutes, until soft &
lightly caramelised. Stir occasionally
to prevent sticking.

Add the garlic & stir for 2 minutes.

Add the all the other ingredients
& simmer for 10 minutes.

Allow to cool slightly.

Pass the soup through a mouli
to remove the tomato skins.

Blend until smooth using a
hand blender.

Wheat Free
Gluten Free
Vegetarian

Tomato & Lentil Soup

INGREDIENTS
Serves 4

100g lentils

4 carrots, finely chopped

4 cloves garlic, finely chopped

1 onion, finely chopped

1200g chopped tomatoes
or tomato passata

1 bunch basil leaves

500ml vegetable stock, homemade
(see page 16)

a few twists of freshly ground
black pepper

1 small bunch finely chopped parsley

METHOD

Add all ingredients in a pan &
simmer for about an hour.

Blend until smooth.

⊗ Wheat Free
◉ Gluten Free
◐ Dairy Free
Ⓥ Vegetarian

Tomato, Red Pepper & Lentil Soup

INGREDIENTS
Serves 4

1 onion, chopped

4 red peppers, deseeded & chopped

800g tomatoes

100g red lentils

600ml vegetable stock, homemade
(see page 16)

METHOD

Add all ingredients in a pan & simmer for about 45 minutes.

Blend until smooth.

Wheat Free 🚫
Gluten Free 🚫
Dairy Free 🥛
Vegetarian Ⓥ

Watercress Soup

INGREDIENTS
Serves 8

28g goat's butter
(or 1 tbsp extra virgin olive oil)

2 medium onions, finely chopped

2 bunches watercress
(roughly 220g in total)

1 large potato, roughly chopped

1 tsp nutmeg, grated

a generous pinch ground pink Himalayan rock salt *(to taste)*

a few twists of freshly ground black pepper

1.4ltr vegetable stock, homemade
(see page 16)

4 tbsp goat's milk

METHOD

Soak the watercress for 15 minutes, wash thoroughly in distilled water, drain.

Sauté the onions in the goat's butter (or the olive oil) over a very low heat, for about 20 minutes, until soft & lightly caramelised. Stir occasionally to prevent sticking.

Meanwhile, roughly chop the watercress.

Add the chopped potato to the sautéd onions; continue to sauté for 3 or 4 minutes, stirring occasionally.

Add the salt, pepper, nutmeg, stock & goat's milk.

Bring to the boil & simmer over a low heat for 10 minutes.

Add the watercress; continue to simmer for a further 4 minutes.

Leave to cool slightly. Blend to desired consistency using a hand blender or food processor.

Wheat Free
Gluten Free
V Vegetarian

BREAD&PASTRY

RECIPES
4LIFE

Fighting Back with Food

Basic Bread Recipe

INGREDIENTS
See portion guide below

570ml distilled water

1 tsp blackstrap molasses, honey or maple syrup

28g fresh yeast
(available from the 'in-store bakery' in most large supermarkets)

900g flour *(450g wholemeal spelt, 225g white spelt, 225g wholemeal wheat)*

2 tsp pink Himalayan rock salt

2 tsp extra virgin olive oil

¼ tsp pure vitamin C powder
('ascorbic acid' helps bread to rise)

1 handful sunflower seeds or flaxseeds

Makes approx:
1 large loaf;
12 to 16 rolls;
2 large pizza bases & a small cob loaf, or 6 large pizza bases.

Cooking times at:
180°C/350°F/Gas Mark 4:

2lb loaf:	**35 minutes***
Cob loaf:	**25 minutes***
Bread rolls:	**15 minutes***
Baguettes:	**20 minutes***
Pizza bases:	**8 minutes***

*Cooking times can vary depending on the type & age of your oven & the size & thickness of each item.

Test to check that the loaves & rolls are cooked through by tapping them on the base. A hollow sound means they are done.

Basic Bread Recipe

METHOD

Boil 200ml of the distilled or filtered water, pour into a measuring jug with the molasses, honey or maple syrup & stir to dissolve.

Top up to 570ml with the remaining cold water & stir.

Pour into a large bowl, add the crumbled yeast & stir to dissolve.

Weigh & mix your choice of flours, with the vitamin C.

Sieve roughly half the flour on top of the water mixture, sprinkle on the salt & drizzle over the olive oil. Sieve the rest of the flour on top. At this point you can also add the sunflower or flaxseeds.

Mix with a large wooden spoon.

Turn out onto a well floured surface & knead by hand for 5 minutes OR alternatively, mix for 2 minutes using the dough hook attachment of your mixer.

Place the dough in a large bowl & cover with a damp tea-towel & leave in a warm place to rise (prove) for 1 hour.

Lightly grease the bread tins & baking trays with olive oil.

Turn out onto a well floured board & knead (knock back) for 2 minutes.

Shape into rolls, pizza bases, baguettes, cob loaves, put into bread tins as required. The pizza bases need to be rolled out very thinly as they will rise to double the thickness.

Leave to rise (prove) for a second time, for approx. 1 hour, or until doubled in size.

Bake in a preheated oven.

Suitable for freezing.

Dairy Free
Vegetarian

Butternut Squash Bread

INGREDIENTS
Makes 1 loaf

375g butternut squash

300g gluten free bread flour

2 tsp gluten free baking powder

1 tsp herbs

2 cloves garlic, finely chopped

2 tbsp organic olive oil

***Can be served with homemade
baked beans (see page 44).***

METHOD

Pre-heat the oven to 200°C/400°F/
Gas Mark 6.

Bake a small whole squash for
45 minutes & allow to cool for
30 minutes.

Remove the skin & seeds; place
in a clean bowl & mash.

Weigh 375g of mashed squash
in a clean bowl; add the flour,
seasoning, oil & baking powder.

Place on a floured board
& knead until soft & spongy
*(add a little more flour if too sticky
or a little water if too dry)*.

Place the dough in a small loaf tin
& bake for 30-35 minutes; insert
a knife into the loaf if it comes out
'clean' the bread is done.

◉ Wheat Free
◉ Gluten Free
◉ Dairy Free
Ⓥ Vegetarian

Gluten Free, Dairy Free, Egg Free Bread

INGREDIENTS
Serves 4

2 cups rice flour

1 cup tapioca starch

1/3 cup of trehalose (optional)

1 tbsp xanthan gum

2 tsp cream of tartar

1 tsp bicarbonate of soda

½ cup organic olive oil

1½ - 2 cups water

METHOD

Pre-heat oven to 190ºC/375ºF /Gas Mark 5.

Combine all the dry ingredients together in a large bowl.

Add the oil & 1 cup of water to the ingredients & mix with a spoon.

Using dough hooks on an electric hand mixer slowly add water until the consistency is toothpaste-like.

Place in a 2lb loaf tin & shape (it won't fill the tin so shape by squashing the mixture with a spoon).

Bake in oven for approx 50 minutes, turning once.

Turn out & wait until cool before cutting.

Suitable for freezing.

To find more information on trehalose or to purchase for your use in this recipe, please visit www.buytrehalose.co.uk

Wheat Free
Gluten Free
Dairy Free
Vegetarian

Pastry For Pasties & Pies

INGREDIENTS
Makes 1 serving

220g white spelt flour

135g goat's butter

juice of 1 orange

60ml filtered or distilled water

a pinch of pink Himalayan rock salt

METHOD

Sieve the flour into a bowl which will fit into the freezer.

Add the goat's butter, chopped into 2.5cm pieces & freeze for 20 minutes.

Squeeze 1 orange & mix the juice with the water & refrigerate for 20 minutes.

Using a food processor, pulse-blend the flour & butter until you can't see any lumps of butter then transfer it into a bowl.

Add the orange juice & water & stir with a spoon until it forms into dough.

Turn the dough out onto a floured surface & shape briefly to coat the dough lightly in flour.

Put the dough back in the fridge for 20 minutes before using.

Ⓥ Vegetarian

Short Crust Pastry

INGREDIENTS
Makes 1 serving

285g flour
*(145g white spelt,
140g finely ground
wholemeal wheat flour)*

140g goat's butter, cold

a pinch of pink Himalayan rock salt

3 tbsp distilled or filtered cold water

METHOD

Sieve the flour & salt into a large mixing bowl.

Add the butter cut into small pieces; rub the butter into the flour, until it resembles fine breadcrumbs.

Gradually mix in small amounts of cold water, just enough to bring the mixture together to form a dough.

Leave the dough for 20 minutes on a floured work surface, or in the fridge, before using.

If you're using the pastry to line a flan dish, roll out the pastry,
line your dish then leave it to rest for 20 minutes in the dish.
The pastry will then be much less likely to crack.

Vegetarian **v**

SNACKS&
LUNCHBOXES

RECIPES
4LIFE

Fighting Back with Food

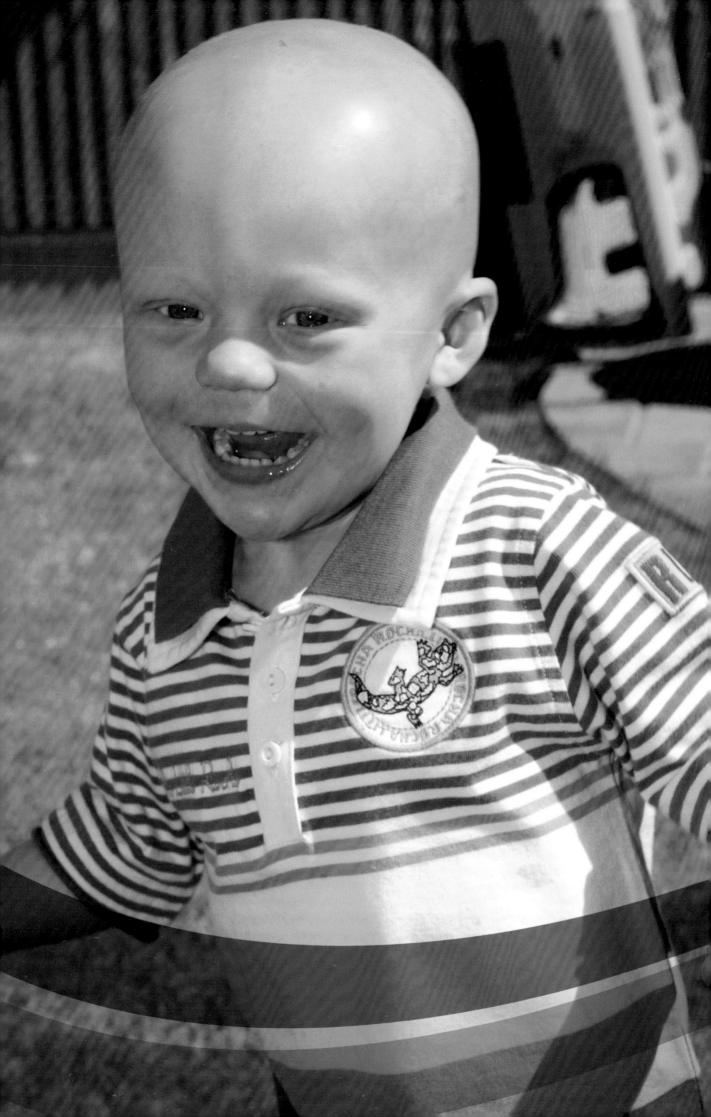

Alfie's "Eggy Knock Knock"

INGREDIENTS
Serves 1

2 organic eggs

a splash of oat milk

knob of coconut oil

METHOD

Beat the eggs & milk together in a bowl.

Heat the oil in a saucepan; add the egg/milk mixture & beat all the time whilst on the heat.

Cook until light & fluffy.

This dish was Alfie's favourite lunchtime snack or in fact, anytime snack. Alfie named this dish as he would watch & help prepare this . We would "Knock Knock" the eggs to break them.

He always knew what he wanted & an "Eggy Knock Knock" demand was one he would always ask...

...Mainly when we were in places with nowhere to prepare!

Wheat Free
Dairy Free
Vegetarian

Baked Beans In Tomato Sauce

INGREDIENTS
Serves 5

400ml tomato sauce, homemade
(see page 15)

335g haricot beans, dry weight

80g red kidney beans *(optional)*

½ tsp pink Himalayan rock salt

a few twists of freshly ground black pepper

2-4 tsp maple syrup
(sweeten to taste)

METHOD

Soak the beans overnight & then follow the cooking instructions on the packets of dried beans OR If using a pressure cooker, cover the beans in plenty of boiling filtered or distilled water & leave to soak for 1 hour. Drain off the soak water & put the beans into the pressure cooker with at least 1ltr of distilled water & bring to the boil. Following the instructions for your pressure cooker, cook for 25 minutes.

Drain the beans through a sieve & add to your home made tomato sauce.

Place in an oven proof dish with the lid on.

Bake them in the oven at 170°C/335°F/Gas Mark 3, for about 25 minutes.

To save time, you can alternatively heat the beans through in a saucepan over a low heat.

⊗ Wheat Free
◉ Gluten Free
◉ Dairy Free
Ⓥ Vegetarian

Butternut Squash Fritters

INGREDIENTS
Serves 6

METHOD

**4 cups butternut squash,
peeled & grated**

1 small onion, peeled & grated

3 organic eggs, whisked

coconut oil, for frying

In a large bowl mix together the
squash, onion & eggs.

Use your hands to make 5cm patties.

Heat the oil in a large skillet & fry
the patties over a medium heat until
golden brown & crispy on both sides.

Remove patties & place on a paper
towel lined plate to drain excess oil.

Repeat steps 2 to 4 until all the
mixture is used.

Wheat Free
Gluten Free
Dairy Free
Vegetarian

45

Carrot & Onion Fritters

INGREDIENTS
Serves 6

3 cups carrot, peeled & grated

3 spring onions, finely chopped

3 organic eggs, whisked

½ tsp Himalayan rock salt

½ tsp rice flour

coconut oil, for frying

METHOD

In a large bowl mix together the carrot, spring onion & eggs.

Stir in salt & rice flour.

Heat the oil in a large skillet.

Scoop large tablespoonfuls of the batter into the skillet & fry over a medium heat until golden brown & crispy on both sides.

Remove the cooked fritters & place on a paper towel lined plate to drain excess oil.

Repeat the process until all the mixture is used.

Wheat Free
Gluten Free
Dairy Free
V Vegetarian

Dry Fried Eggy Bread

INGREDIENTS
Serves 4

8 eggs, beaten

A splash of rice or oat milk

4 thick slices bread, homemade *(see page 34)* **or gluten free bread** *(see page37)*

1 tbsp chopped fresh coriander *(to garnish)*

METHOD

Beat the eggs with the milk.

Pour the mixture onto a serving plate.

Lay the bread on top & allow to soak for a few minutes. Turn the bread over & wait until the bread has soaked up most of the egg.

Heat a frying pan & when really hot add the egg soaked bread. Gently dry fry the bread until golden brown & the egg is cooked through.

You could cut out shapes for children using pastry cutters or serve whole.

Dairy Free
Vegetarian Ⓥ

Fritata With Cherry Tomatoes & Baby Spinach

INGREDIENTS
Serves 2-3

6 organic eggs

1 tsp organic olive oil

200g cherry tomatoes

350g baby spinach

chopped fresh basil

chopped fresh parsley

Can be eaten cold – ideal for lunch-boxes.

METHOD

Preheat the oven to 200°/400°F/ Gas Mark 6.

Whisk the eggs with 2 tbsp distilled water.

Heat the oil in a cast iron pan or fritata plate or frying pan with 1 tbsp of water. Add the tomatoes & spinach & cook until spinach begins to wilt. Sprinkle over the herbs.

Pour in the eggs & transfer to the preheated oven.

Bake for 10-12 minutes until well risen & golden brown.

Serve in slices & serve with a side salad.

🌾 Wheat Free
Ⓢ Gluten Free
Ⓓ Dairy Free
Ⓥ Vegetarian

Garlic Cheese On Toast

INGREDIENTS
Serves 1

1 slice of bread, homemade
(see page 34)

1–2 tsp goat's butter

1 tbsp hummus, home made
(see page 13)

**55g hard goat's cheese,
finely sliced or grated**

METHOD

Toast the bread.

Preheat the grill to a medium heat.

Spread the toast with the goat's butter & then the hummus.

Top with the sliced or grated goat's cheese.

Place under the grill until the cheese has melted.

Serve with a colourful salad tossed in salad dressing.

Vegetarian **v**

Nut Butter Sandwiches

INGREDIENTS
Serves 1

115g chopped nuts

2 tbsp raisins

A little organic olive oil or walnut oil

2 slices bread, homemade, per child
(see page 34)

METHOD

Blend the nuts & raisins together in a food processor to make a thick paste. This will take some time.

Add a little oil to get the right consistency & to help the blending process.

Spread one slice of the bread with some of the nut butter. Top with other slice & cut into four.

Nut Butter can be stored in an airtight jar in the fridge for up to 2 weeks.

🌀 Dairy Free
Ⓥ Vegetarian

Sage & Onion Savoury Scones

INGREDIENTS
Makes 12

75g maize flour

75g gram flour

75g quinoa flour

2 tbsp trehalose

pinch of Himalayan rock salt

1½ tsp cream of tartar

½ tsp bicarbonate of soda

1 tsp xanthan gum

2 shallots or 1 small onion, finely chopped

1 tsp dried sage

55g goat's butter

150ml rice milk

METHOD

Preheat the oven to 220ºC/425ºF/ Gas Mark 7.

Sift the flour into a bowl & mix in all dry ingredients including the dried sage.

Add the butter & rub into the flour to resemble 'breadcumbs'

Add the milk slowly with the chopped onion to make a smooth dough.

Let the dough rest for 5 minutes; roll out on a lightly floured surface until approximately 2cm thick.

Cut with a 5cm pastry cutter; dust with flour & place on a greased baking tray.

Bake for 10 to 12 minutes.

Wheat Free
Gluten Free
Vegetarian

SALADS

RECIPES
4 LIFE

Fighting Back with Food

Asparagus & Avocado Salad

INGREDIENTS
Serves 4

METHOD

225g asparagus spears

2 avocados

2 tbsp lemon juice

2 tbsp sesame seeds, lightly toasted

Dressing:

1 tsp wholegrain mustard

1 tsp honey

2 tbsp balsamic vinegar

Trim the asparagus spears. Steam for 3 minutes. They should still be quite crunchy. Drain & allow them to cool.

Cut the avocados in half, remove the stone & peel. Dice the flesh & toss immediately in the lemon juice to prevent it from going brown.

Remove the avocado from the lemon juice & mix with the asparagus spears & sesame seeds.

Mix the dressing ingredients in a small bowl & then drizzle over the salad. Toss well then serve.

Wheat Free
Gluten Free
Dairy Free
Vegetarian **V**

Carrot, Coriander & Cashew Nut Salad

INGREDIENTS
Serves 4

85g cashews

4 medium sized carrots

juice of half a lemon

4 tbsp fresh coriander leaves, chopped

freshly ground black pepper

METHOD

Lightly toast the cashews by placing under a hot grill or in a preheated oven for a few minutes until pale golden colour. Set aside to cool.

Peel & grate the carrots. Transfer to a mixing bowl, add lemon juice, & stir well.

Add the cashews & chopped coriander leaves. Toss well & season to taste with the black pepper.

- ⊗ Wheat Free
- ⊗ Gluten Free
- ⊗ Dairy Free
- Ⓥ Vegetarian

Chickpea & Red Pepper Salad With Walnuts

INGREDIENTS
Serves 4

400g chickpeas, soaked & cooked

1 red onion, thinly sliced

1 red pepper, de-seeded & sliced

12 black olives, pitted

100g watercress

85g walnuts, lightly toasted

Dressing:

3 tbsp coconut oil or organic olive oil

2 tbsp balsamic vinegar

1 garlic clove, crushed

½ tbsp dijon mustard

METHOD

In a large bowl, mix together the chickpeas, onion, pepper & olives.

Place the dressing ingredients in a bottle or screw top glass jar & shake until combined. Add half of the dressing to the chickpea salad & mix until well combined.

Toss the watercress with the remaining dressing. Transfer to a serving plate.

Top with the chickpea salad & sprinkle with the toasted walnuts.

Wheat Free
Gluten Free
Dairy Free
Vegetarian V

Energy Salad With Garlic & Honey Dressing

INGREDIENTS
Serves 1

a few assorted leafy green salad leaves

1 small carrot, grated or cut into batons

1 small handful of raisins

1 small handful of bean sprouts

a few slices of cucumber

1 handful of sunflower seeds, toasted

a couple of cherry tomatoes, halved

Garlic & honey dressing:

1 garlic clove, crushed

½ tsp honey

½ tsp dijon mustard

1 tbsp apple cider vinegar

2 tbsp flaxseed oil or extra virgin olive oil

METHOD

Arrange the salad decoratively in a bowl.

Mix together the garlic, honey & mustard & then add the vinegar & oil. Mix well & pour over the salad.

SALADS

Wheat Free
Gluten Free
Dairy Free
V Vegetarian

Feta, Watermelon & Pumpkin Seed Salad

INGREDIENTS
Serves 4

4 tbsp lightly toasted pumpkin seeds

half a watermelon, rind removed, sliced into thin wedges

200g feta cheese

4 tbsp black olives, pitted & halved

freshly ground black pepper

METHOD

Lightly toast the pumpkin seeds in a dry frying pan for a few minutes until they start to pop.
Leave to cool.

Place the watermelon on a large platter.

Crumble the feta cheese over the top & sprinkle with the olives & pumpkin seeds.

Season with black pepper.

Can be made in advance, but keep chilled. ❄

Wheat Free 🌾
Gluten Free 🚫
Vegetarian Ⓥ

Goat's Cheese, Pear & Pecan Salad

INGREDIENTS
Serves 1

1 slice firm goat's cheese
(approx. 75-100g) **sliced
or crumbled into chunks**

1 ripe pear, cored & thinly sliced

1 tbsp pecan halves
(roughly chopped if you prefer)

**1 little gem lettuce, washed, drained
& torn into bite-sized pieces**

**a good couple of handfuls of
watercress roughly chopped or torn**

METHOD

Scatter the cheese, pear slices & nuts over a bed of lettuce & watercress.

The fat & flavour from the nuts & cheese mean that you shouldn't need extra dressing.

Ⓦ Wheat Free
Ⓖ Gluten Free
Ⓥ Vegetarian

Greek Salad With Fennel & Mint

INGREDIENTS
Serves 4

1 romaine *(cos)* **lettuce**

1 cucumber

2 large tomatoes

1 green, red or orange pepper

1 red onion

115g black kalamata olives

175g feta cheese

For the Dressing:

4 tbsp coconut oil or organic olive oil

juice of 1 lemon

a small bunch flat leaf parsley, chopped

a little Himalayan rock salt

a few twists of freshly ground black pepper

METHOD

Cut the lettuce in wide ribbons.

Cut the cucumber lengthways in half & then half again & then slice thickly. Cut the tomatoes into quarters.

Remove the seeds from the pepper & slice it thinly.

Slice the onion thinly.

Put the prepared vegetables into a large bowl. Add the feta cheese & olives.

Whisk the dressing ingredients together in a small bowl.

Pour the dressing over the salad & toss well.

Wheat Free
Gluten Free
Vegetarian

61

Marinated Tofu & Cashew Nut Salad

INGREDIENTS
Serves 2

250g plain tofu

For the Marinade:

1 level tsp mustard

2.5cm piece ginger

1 pressed garlic clove

1 tsp honey

1 tbsp organic olive oil

Himalayan rock salt

freshly ground black pepper

salad leaves

10cm piece cucumber

2 large tomatoes

½ yellow pepper

2 handfuls bean sprouts

1 handful cashew nuts

organic olive oil *(for dressing)*

2 tbsp gluten free flour

2 tbsp organic olive oil

METHOD

Cube the tofu & press firmly with kitchen paper to remove excess moisture.

Mix the marinade ingredients together & season.

Toss the marinade with the tofu & leave for 2 hours or longer.

Place the salad leaves in two individual salad bowls.

Cut the cucumber, tomatoes, pepper & bean sprouts & cashew nuts onto the salad leaves. Saving a few cashew nuts & some pepper to garnish.

Dress the salads with olive oil.

Remove the tofu from the marinade & toss it in the flour until lightly coated.

Sauté the tofu in 2 tbsp of olive oil over a medium heat, turning regularly until golden brown.

Pile the warm tofu onto the salads, garnish with the cashew nuts & pepper & serve at once.

- Wheat Free
- Gluten Free
- Dairy Free
- **V** Vegetarian

Roasted Butternut Squash & Feta Salad

INGREDIENTS
Serves 6

700g butternut squash, peeled, deseeded & cut into chunks

6 beetroots, trimmed & quartered

8 whole garlic cloves, unpeeled

1 tbsp organic olive oil

1 tbsp chilli flakes

2 tbsp pumpkin seeds

200g mixed salad leaves

110g Feta cheese, crumbled

For the dressing:

2 tbsp extra virgin olive oil

2 tbsp balsamic vinegar

METHOD

Preheat the oven to 200°C/400°F/ Gas Mark 6. Toss the butternut squash, beetroot & garlic in a roasting tin with the olive oil. Sprinkle over the chilli flakes & roast for 30 minutes, turning occasionally, until the vegetables are softened.

Meanwhile, brown the pumpkin seeds by dry frying them in a frying pan, moving them around the pan for 2-3 minutes until they just change colour & begin popping. Set aside.

Remove the squash & beetroot from the oven & leave to cool slightly.

For the dressing, pop the garlic cloves from their skins *(they should slide out easily)* & mash the flesh with the olive oil & vinegar.

To serve, arrange the salad leaves on serving plates, top with the butternut squash & beetroot & crumble over the Feta.

Sprinkle over the pumpkin seeds & the salad dressing.

Wheat Free 🌾
Gluten Free 🌾
Vegetarian Ⓥ

Roasted Pepper Salad With Salsa

INGREDIENTS
Serves 2

METHOD

4 mixed peppers

1 large onion

1 tbsp olive oil

salad leaves

225g cooked brown rice

4 tbsp beans eg. cannellini

4 tbsp sweetcorn

coriander to garnish

Salsa Sauce:

1 avocado

7.5cm piece cucumber

½-1 green chilli

1 tbsp lemon juice

4 heaped tbsp soya or goat yoghurt

2 tbsp chopped coriander

2 tbsp water

a pinch of Himalayan rock salt

a few twists of freshly ground black pepper

Quarter the peppers & remove the seeds & stalks. Peel the onion & cut into 8 segments. Toss the peppers & onions gently in olive oil to coat & place on a baking tray. Roast, uncovered, at 200°C/400°F/ Gas Mark 6 for 20-25 minutes or until the vegetables are just cooked. Leave to cool.

Line two individual salad bowls with the salad leaves.

Combine the rice, beans & sweetcorn & pile on top of the leaves.

To make the salsa sauce, finely dice the avocado, cucumber & chilli & mix with the lemon juice, yoghurt, chopped coriander & water. Season to taste with salt & pepper.

Pile the salsa on top of the rice, leaving a little rice visible around the edges.

Peel the skins from the peppers & pile these & the onions on top of the salad.

Garnish with coriander & serve.

SALADS

Wheat Free
Gluten Free
V Vegetarian

Tropical Chicken Salad

INGREDIENTS
Serves 4

mixed salad leaves
(include watercress)

2 handfuls beansprouts

20 chunks fresh pineapple

1 handful walnuts

2 chicken breasts

1 tbsp organic olive oil

For the dressing:

4 tbsp chopped pineapple

4 tbsp fresh tarragon

1 rounded tsp mustard

3 tbsp organic olive oil

a pinch of Himalayan rock salt

a few twists of freshly ground black pepper

METHOD

Make two salads in separate salad bowls using the salad leaves, walnuts, beansprouts & pineapple. Save a few walnut & pineapple for a garnish.

Whisk together the dressing ingredients.

Cut the chicken breasts into bite size pieces & sweat these in the olive oil until brown & cooked through.

Pile the warm chicken on top of the salads, drizzle the dressing over & garnish with the remaining pineapple & walnuts. Serve at once.

Wheat Free
Gluten Free
Dairy Free

PASTIES, PIES, PIZZA & QUICHE

RECIPES 4 LIFE

Fighting Back with Food

Cheese & Onion Pasties

INGREDIENTS
Makes 6 Pasties

1 quantity of pastry for pasties & pies
(see page 52)

3 medium onions, finely chopped

25g goat's butter

1 tbsp extra virgin olive oil

135g hard goat's cheese

1½ tbsp white spelt flour

170ml goat's milk

a pinch of pink Himalayan rock salt

a few twists of freshly ground black pepper

METHOD

Sauté the onions in the goat's butter & olive oil, over a very low heat, for about 30 minutes, until soft & lightly caramelised, stirring to prevent sticking.

Add the flour & stir.

Gradually stir in the milk to make a sauce, then add the cheese & seasoning; stir again.

Allow the mixture to cool completely before using it to fill your pasties.

Divide the pastry into 6 equal pieces & roll them out into circular or rectangular shapes.

Divide the filling equally between them, putting the filling in the centre of each circle.

Dampen the edges of the pastry with a little water & join the pastry together over the filling.

Make a small hole in each pasty & glaze with beaten egg; Bake in a preheated oven at 180°C/350°F/ Gas Mark 4 for about 20 minutes.

Vegetarian Ⓥ

Cheese & Onion Quiche

INGREDIENTS
Makes 1 Quiche

1 portion of short crust pastry
(see page 39)

1 tbsp extra virgin olive oil

1 large onion, finely chopped

**½ red pepper,
de-seeded & chopped**

7 organic eggs, beaten

285ml goat's milk

**a pinch of pink
Himalayan rock salt**

METHOD

Grease a flan dish, 28 cm in diameter, with the olive oil.

Roll out the pastry, re-flouring the surface to prevent sticking.

Line the flan dish; Press into the edges of the flan dish removing the excess pastry from around the top of the dish; Leave to rest for 20 minutes.

Gently heat the olive oil in a heavy based pan over the lowest possible heat.

Add the onion & sauté for approx 20 minutes, until sweet & starting to caramelize, stirring occasionally to prevent sticking, add the red pepper after 10 minutes.

Pre-heat the oven to 180°C/350°F/ Gas Mark 4.

Cover the pastry with greaseproof paper & then cover it with a layer of baking beans or rice. Bake in a pre-heated oven for 8-10 minutes.

Turn the oven down to 160°C/320°F/ Gas Mark 3.

Beat the eggs, milk & seasoning together & add the grated cheese.

Patch up any cracks in the pastry case with the left-over pastry scraps.

Spread the cooled onions plus the red pepper, over the base of the pastry case.

Pour in the egg mixture & spread out the cheese evenly over the top.

Return to the oven & bake for approx 25 minutes, until set & golden.

Ⓥ Vegetarian

Homity Pie

INGREDIENTS
Makes 1 Pie

1 portion of short crust pastry
(see page 38)

1 tbsp extra virgin olive oil

2 large onions, finely chopped

**3 large potatoes, peeled & chopped
into 2.5cm cubes**

285g hard goat's cheese, grated

4 cloves garlic, crushed

1 bunch fresh parsley, chopped

1 tbsp goat's milk

½ tsp pink Himalayan rock salt

**a few twists
of freshly ground
black pepper**

METHOD

Grease a flan dish *(28 cm in diameter)* with the olive oil.

Roll out the dough, re-flouring the surface to prevent sticking.

Line the flan dish; Press into the edges of the flan dish removing the excess pastry from around the top of the dish; Leave to rest for 20 minutes.

Pre-heat the oven to 180°C/350°F/ Gas Mark 4.

Cover the pastry with greaseproof paper & then cover it with a layer of baking beans or rice. Bake in a pre-heated oven for 8-10 minutes.

For the Filling:

Prepare the potatoes & cook in boiling water until tender, drain & allow to cool slightly.

Gently sauté the onions in the olive oil until soft & starting to caramelise. Stir occasionally to prevent sticking.

In a large bowl combine the potatoes, sautéed onions, parsley, milk, garlic, seasoning & half the cheese. Mix well.

Add the mixture to the pastry lined flan dish.

Sprinkle the remaining cheese over the top.

Bake in the oven for 25–30 minutes at 170°C/335°F/Gas Mark 3.

Vegetarian Ⓥ

Pizza

INGREDIENTS
For 2 Pizzas

1/3 of the quantity of bread dough 'Basic Bread Recipe' *(see page 34)*

8 tbsp tomato sauce, homemade *(see page 15)*

2 heaped tbsp fresh basil, roughly chopped

1 small red onion

½ red pepper, thinly sliced

a covering of hard goat's cheese, thinly sliced or grated

METHOD

To cook Fresh:

Cover the pizzas with a layer of the tomato sauce, using the back of a metal spoon.

Add layers of the toppings, finally covering with a layer of sliced goat's cheese.

Bake for approx 10 minutes at 180°C/350°F/Gas Mark 4, until the base is cooked through & the cheese is bubbling & golden brown.

To cook for Freezing:

Cook the bases for 8 minutes at 180°C/350°F/Gas Mark 4.

Place on a wire rack & leave until cool.

Cover both pizzas with a thin layer of the tomato sauce using the back of a metal spoon.

Add layers of toppings, finally covering with a layer of sliced goat's cheese.

Place the pizza on large plates & freeze.

Once frozen, place individually in large brown paper bags *(available from some health food shops)* & put back in the freezer.

Cook from frozen for 15-20 minutes at 180°C/350°F/Gas Mark 4.

PASTIES, PIES, PIZZA & QUICHE

V Vegetarian

Sweet Potato & French Bean Pasties

INGREDIENTS
Makes 8 Pasties

1 quantity of pastry for pasties & pies *(see page 38)*

1 tbsp extra virgin olive oil

½ medium onion, finely chopped

1 clove garlic, crushed

1 tbsp ginger, freshly grated

¼-½ tsp chilli powder

1 tsp turmeric

1 tsp ground cumin

2 tsp ground coriander

½ tsp mustard powder

1 medium sweet potato, *(cooked & finely diced)*

110g french beans, chopped into 1cm lengths

2 tbsp vegetable stock, homemade *(see page 16)* **or filtered water**

2 tsp coconut milk

a pinch of pink Himalayan rock salt

a few twists of freshly ground black pepper

1 egg, beaten *(optional, for glazing)*

METHOD

Gently heat the olive oil in a heavy based pan over the lowest possible heat.

Add the onion & sauté in the oil for approx 15 minutes, until sweet & starting to caramelize. Stir occasionally to prevent sticking.

Meanwhile, prepare & steam the diced sweet potato & beans.

Add the garlic & ginger to the onions & stir for 2 minutes.

Add the spices & stir for another minute.

Add the diced sweet potato, beans, stock or water, coconut milk & seasoning & cook gently for 4–5 minutes.

Allow the mixture to cool & add extra seasoning to taste.

Preheat the oven to 170°C/325°F/ Gas Mark 3.

Roll out the pastry into 8 circles & divide the filling equally between them, putting the filling in the centre of each circle.

Dampen the edges of the pastry with a little water & join pastry together over the filling & make a small hole in each pasty; glaze with beaten egg if desired.

Bake for about 20 minutes.

These can be frozen before cooking. If baking from frozen, bake in a preheated oven for approximately 30 minutes.

Vegetarian **V**

VEGETABLE DISHES

RECIPES
4LIFE

Fighting Back with Food

Baked Bhajis

INGREDIENTS
Serves 4

1 tbsp organic olive oil
(not extra virgin)

2 red onion, diced

2 garlic cloves, crushed

4 tsp curry powder

150g baby leaf spinach

**275g dried chickpeas,
soaked & cooked**

**2 heaped tbsp finely
chopped coriander**

2 tsp Himalayan rock salt

2 medium organic eggs, beaten

*Can be made in advance,
suitable for freezing.*

METHOD

Preheat the oven to 180°C/350°F/
Gas Mark 4. Line a baking tray with
non-stick paper.

Heat the oil in a small pan & sweat
the onion & garlic with the curry
powder for around 5 minutes to
soften. Add the spinach to the pan &
stir to wilt for a further minute or so.

Place all the other ingredients except
the eggs in a food processor & blend
until fairly smooth & combined. Mix in
the egg, shape into 16 patties & place
on the tray.

Cook the Bhajis for around 25
minutes or until firm to the touch.

Wheat Free 🚫
Gluten Free 🌾
Dairy Free 🥛
Vegetarian Ⓥ

Baked Carrot French Fries

INGREDIENTS
Serves 4

6 large carrots

2 tbsp organic olive oil

½ tsp Himalayan rock salt

METHOD

Pre-heat the oven to 220°C/425°F/ Gas Mark 7.

Wash the carrots, in filtered water & dry; remove top & any blemishes.

Cut each carrot into 5cm long sections & each section into thin sticks.

In a large bowl coat the carrot sticks with the oil & salt.

Place the chips on a baking tray, preferably stoneware *(avoid non-stick)*.

Bake in the oven for about 18-22 minutes until carrots are browned, turning after 10 minutes.

Wheat Free
Gluten Free
Dairy Free
V Vegetarian

VEGETABLE DISHES

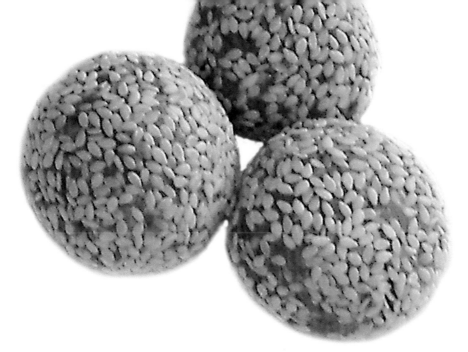

Baked Falafel

INGREDIENTS
Serves 4

275g dried chickpeas, cooked

4 garlic cloves, crushed

4 tsp tahini

10 spring onions, roughly sliced

50g sesame seeds

4 tsp ground cumin

2 tsp ground coriander

2 tbsp flat leaf parsley, finely chopped

2 tsp Himalayan rock salt

2 tsp freshly ground black pepper

2 medium organic eggs

60g sesame seeds for coating

Can be made in advance, suitable for freezing.

METHOD

Preheat the oven to 200°C/400°F/ Gas Mark 6.

Place all ingredients bar the salt, pepper, egg & sesame seeds in a food processor & blend until fairly smooth & combined. Taste & season accordingly. Mix in the beaten egg & shape into 16 golf sized balls.

Put the sesame seeds on a plate & roll the balls in them. This is a bit fiddly, so you may prefer to scatter the seeds over each side of the falafel. It might be necessary to then reshape the falafel in your hand.

Place the balls on the baking tray & cook for 20-25 minutes or until just golden on top & firm to the touch.

Delicious served with a dollop of hummus *(see page 13)*.

Wheat Free
Gluten Free
Dairy Free
Vegetarian **V**

Beanie Chilli

INGREDIENTS
Serves 6-8

1 tbsp extra virgin olive oil

1 large onion, finely chopped

2 cloves garlic, crushed

400ml tomato sauce, homemade
(see page 15)

275g dried beans
(a mix of haricot, red kidney, black-eye, chick peas & butter beans)

1 red pepper

½-1 green chilli, fresh or ½-1 tsp of chilli powder

110g sweetcorn, frozen

1 red pepper, chopped *(optional)*

1 small courgette

650ml passata

½ tsp ground pink Himalayan rock salt

a few twists of freshly ground black pepper *(to taste)*

1 tsp maple syrup *(to taste)*

METHOD

To cook the beans:

Soak the beans overnight & follow the cooking instructions on the packets of dried beans/peas OR To pressure cook, cover the beans in plenty of boiling filtered or distilled water & leave to soak for 1 hour. Drain off the soak water & put the beans into the pressure cooker with at least 1ltr of distilled water, bring to the boil. cook for 25 minutes, following the instructions for your pressure cooker.

Prepare & cook the beans.

Sauté the onions in the olive oil, over a very low heat, for about 20 minutes, until soft & lightly caramelised, stirring occasionally to prevent sticking.

Crush the garlic *(10 minutes before using)*.

Add the red pepper, if using, 10 minutes after the onions.

Add the crushed garlic & chopped chilli for the final couple of minutes of sautéing, stirring continuously.

Add the homemade tomato sauce, cooked beans & all the other vegetables.

Simmer gently on the cooker top for about 20 minutes.

Serve with quinoa (pronounced 'keen-wah'), brown basmati rice, baked potato, baked sweet potato (orange fleshed) or 'chunky oven chips' with a fresh green salad.

Wheat Free
Gluten Free
Dairy Free
V Vegetarian

Butternut Squash Risotto

INGREDIENTS
Serves 4

For the Risotto:

1 tbsp organic olive oil

1 small onion or 2 shallots, finely chopped

1 carrot, finely chopped

1 garlic clove, finely chopped

250g risotto rice

50ml grape juice diluted with 50ml distilled water

1ltr vegetable stock *(organic vegetable bouillon)*

1 small butternut squash, chopped into small cubes

For the Pesto:

2 large handfuls basil leaves

1 garlic clove *(crush before adding if using a processor)*

pinch of Himalayan rock salt

large handful of roasted pine nuts

juice of ½ a lemon

100ml organic olive oil

METHOD

Grind the basil & garlic with the salt in a Pestle & Mortar. When you have a paste, add the pine nuts & grind again. Finally mix in the lemon & the olive oil. If you use a food processor, throw in all the ingredients & blitz. This will give a chunkier texture.

To make the risotto heat the oil in a heavy based saucepan with high sides & gently fry the onion, celery, carrot & garlic. When these are soft turn up the heat & add the rice stirring for 4-5 minutes until it's coated in oil.

Add the grape juice & water which should sizzle when you pour it into the pan & allow it to be soaked up. When the pan is almost dry start to add 300ml of the stock & the butternut squash. Add another splash when the liquid has almost been soaked up. Stir steadily & fairly constantly until you have used all the stock or risotto rice is cooked & the mixture is nice & loose.

Take the pan off the heat & allow the risotto to rest for a couple of minutes before serving with a little pesto spooned over the top.

VEGETABLE DISHES

Wheat Free
Gluten Free
Dairy Free
Vegetarian Ⓥ

Cashew & Sesame Quinoa

INGREDIENTS
Serves 2

140g quinoa

1 tsp vegetable bouillon powder

3-4 tbsp fresh *(or frozen & thawed)* **petit pois or peas**

2 tbsp cashew nuts

2 tsp sesame oil

1 tbsp tamari sauce

2 tsp lemon juice

1 carrot, julienned *(finely sliced lengthways into matchsticks)*

6 spring onions *(finely sliced on the diagonal)*

freshly ground black pepper

METHOD

Add the quinoa & bouillon powder to a saucepan, cover with double the amount of cold, distilled water & bring to the boil. Cover & simmer for 13 minutes, or until all the water has been absorbed & the quinoa grains are soft & fluffy.

Add the peas & stir through for a couple of minutes then remove from the heat. They will cook or soften slightly in the residual warmth.

Combine with the remaining ingredients, tossing thoroughly to mix all the flavours & allow the quinoa to absorb the liquid seasonings.

Wheat Free
Gluten Free
Dairy Free
V Vegetarian

Cheesy Vegetable Pie

INGREDIENTS
Serves 6-8

Topping:

6 medium potatoes, washed, peeled & quartered

28g goat's butter

3 tbsp goat's milk

a pinch of pink Himalayan rock salt, ground

a few twists of freshly ground black pepper

For the Base:

28g goat's butter

1 tbsp extra virgin olive oil

1 large onion, finely chopped

1 red pepper, diced

80g french beans, trimmed & sliced in 2cm pieces

2 carrots, sliced

a few broccoli florets, small *(optional)*

110g sweetcorn, frozen

165g hard goat's cheese, grated, reserving 28g for sprinkling on the top

40g flour, white spelt

430ml goat's milk

METHOD

Prepare & boil the potatoes until cooked through, about 15 minutes, then drain.

Meanwhile, sauté the onions in the olive oil, over a very low heat, for about 15 minutes, until soft & slightly caramelised, stirring occasionally to prevent sticking.

Prepare & lightly steam the beans, carrots & broccoli, for 3–5 minutes.

Add the chopped red pepper to the onions & continue to sauté for a further 5 minutes.

While still over a low heat, sprinkle the flour over the onions & red peppers and stir in, making a roux.

Preheat the oven to 170°C/325°F/ Gas Mark 3.

Gradually add the milk, stirring all the time to prevent the sauce from becoming lumpy, until the sauce has thickened.

Add the grated cheese, sweet corn & steamed vegetables & season to taste.

Put the vegetable mixture in a casserole dish.

Mash the potatoes with the goat's butter, goat's milk, salt & pepper and spread the mashed potato over the vegetables.

Sprinkle the remaining grated cheese over the top.

Bake in the oven for 20–25 minutes.

Vegetarian **v**

Chickpea & Cauliflower Curry

INGREDIENTS
Serves 4

METHOD

2 tbsp coconut oil or organic olive oil

3 tbsp medium curry paste

2 large onions, sliced

½ cauliflower, broken into small florets

400g chickpeas, soaked & cooked

400ml coconut milk

210ml hot vegetable stock

1 tbsp tamari sauce

250g fine green beans

handful of coriander, torn or roughly chopped

a little Himalayan rock salt

Put the oil & the curry paste in a large frying pan or wok & fry the onions over a medium heat for around 5 minutes to soften them. Add the cauliflower & chickpeas to the pan & stir to coat them in the other ingredients.

Pour in the coconut milk, stock & tamari sauce & stir. Bring to the boil, then cover & simmer over a gentle heat for around 30 minutes or until the cauliflower is fairly soft.

Stir in the green beans & cook for another 5 minutes or so until they are tender.

Check the seasoning, add salt if necessary & scatter with the coriander leaves before serving.

Wheat Free
Gluten Free
Dairy Free
V Vegetarian

Chunky Oven Chips

INGREDIENTS
Serves 4

4 medium potatoes or sweet potatoes, peeled

2–3 tbsp extra virgin olive oil

large pinch of pink Himalayan rock salt

METHOD

Pre-heat the oven to 180°C/350°F/ Gas Mark 4.

Wash the potatoes, in filtered water.

Either peel the potatoes or just remove the blemishes *(most of the goodness is just under the skin).*

Cut into chunky, similar sized chip shapes.

Toss the chips in the olive oil, ensuring they are all well coated.

Place the chips on a baking tray, preferably stoneware *(avoid non-stick)* & sprinkle with the pink Himalayan rock salt.

Bake in the oven for about 30 minutes until golden brown, turning after 15 minutes.

Wheat Free
Gluten Free
Dairy Free
Vegetarian

Couscous With Roasted Red Peppers, Tomatoes & Mint

INGREDIENTS
Serves 4

2 tbsp coconut oil or organic olive oil

1 small red pepper

1 small yellow pepper

200g cherry tomatoes, halved

225g couscous

300ml hot vegetable stock
(see page 16) **or distilled water**

400g red kidney beans,
soaked & cooked

a small handful of fresh mint, chopped

Himalayan rock salt

freshly ground black pepper

METHOD

Preheat the oven to 200°C/400°F/ Gas Mark 6.

Remove the seeds from the peppers & cut then into wide strips. Place in a large roasting tin with the cherry tomatoes, drizzle with the oil & toss lightly so that the vegetables are well coated in the oil. Roast in the oven for about 30 minutes until the peppers are slightly tender. Allow to cool then roughly chop the peppers.

Put the couscous in a large bowl & cover with the hot stock or water. Stir briefly, cover & allow to stand for 5 minutes until the stock has been absorbed. Fluff up with a fork.

Add the roast peppers, tomatoes, beans & mint. Season to taste with salt & black pepper.

Dairy Free
V Vegetarian

Creamy Tahini & Vegetable Casserole

INGREDIENTS
Serves 2

2 onions

1 garlic clove

1 tbsp organic olive oil

2 large carrots

1 red pepper

3 rounded tbsp tahini

425ml vegetable stock

200g blackeye beans, soaked & drained

Himalayan rock salt

freshly ground black pepper

1 tbsp chopped fresh parsley & extra parsley to garnish

METHOD

Pre-heat oven to 200ºC/400ºF/Gas Mark 6.

Cut the onion into chunks & press the garlic clove.

Sweat the onion & garlic in the olive oil in a casserole dish until the vegetables begin to soften.

Cut the carrot & pepper into bite size chunks & add to the casserole. Dissolve the tahini in the vegetable stock & add this too.

Add the blackeye beans to the casserole & bake for one hour or until the vegetable are cooked. Don't worry if the mixture looks curdled when you take it out of the oven as it will become creamy when stirred.

Season to taste with salt & pepper & serve garnished with parsley.

VEGETABLE DISHES

Wheat Free
Gluten Free
Dairy Free
Vegetarian

Falafel Burgers

INGREDIENTS
Makes 10

400g chickpeas, soaked & cooked

half a small onion, finely chopped

1 garlic clove, finely chopped

a small handful of chopped
flat leaf parsley

a small handful of chopped coriander

1 tsp ground cumin

1 tsp coriander

½ tsp cinnamon

2 tbsp rice flour & extra
for dusting

200ml coconut oil for frying

METHOD

Put the chickpeas, onion, garlic, herbs, spices & flour in a food processor & blend until smooth.

Flour your hands & shape the mixture into 10 patties.

Heat the oil in a frying until it is nice & hot. Fry the falafels on both sides for 2-3 minutes until golden brown & crispy. Leave them on a sheet of kitchen towel to drain.

Serve with a dollop of hummus *(see page 13)* & guacamole *(see page 10)*, or homemade tomato ketchup *(see page 14)*.

Wheat Free
Gluten Free
Dairy Free
V Vegetarian

Indian Spiced Butternut Squash

INGREDIENTS
Serves 4

950g butternut squash, washed but unpeeled

½ tsp turmeric

1½ tsp ground cumin

1½ tsp ground coriander

1 tsp Himalayan rock salt

2 tbsp tomato puree

1 tbsp organic olive oil

Can be made in advance.

METHOD

Preheat the oven to 200°C/400°F/ Gas Mark 6.

Cut the butternut squash in half lengthways & scrape out all the seeds & pulp with a spoon. Cut each half into four, lengthways, so you have eight long pieces in total.

Mix the turmeric, cumin, coriander, salt, tomato puree & oil together in a bowl, then rub the paste all over the squash until evenly coated.

Place the squash in a roasting dish & cook for 45-60 minutes or until the flesh is soft when pierced or squashed, removing from the oven halfway through to turn the pieces over.

Wheat Free
Gluten Free
Dairy Free
Vegetarian Ⓥ

Kidney Bean Pilaff

INGREDIENTS
Serves 4

METHOD

For the rice:

225g brown rice

1 onion, chopped

600ml vegetable stock, homemade
(see page 16)

2 tbsp tomato puree

420g red kidney beans, soaked & cooked

For the pesto:

25g flat leaf parsley

finely grated zest & juice of 1 lemon

1 tbsp coconut oil or organic olive oil

15g ground almonds

1 tbsp grated parmesan cheese

Himalayan rock salt

freshly ground black pepper

Place the rice in a large saucepan with the chopped onion & stock & bring to the boil. Reduce the heat, cover & simmer for 35-40 minutes, until the rice is tender.

Drain the rice well, & mix in the tomato puree & red kidney beans. In a clean pan, heat the rice mixture gently to warm it through.

Meanwhile, make the pesto. Remove any tough stalks from the parsley & chop the leaves finely. Mix it together with the lemon zest & juice, oil, almonds, parmesan cheese & seasoning.

Add the pesto to the rice mixture. Stir well & heat through.

Serve this pilaff hot, or chill it in the fridge & serve it cold as a rice salad.

Wheat Free
Gluten Free
V Vegetarian

Lentil & Squash Curry

INGREDIENTS
Serves 4

1 tbsp organic olive oil

2 red onions, chopped

4 garlic cloves, crushed

1 medium butternut squash, unpeeled, de-seeded & cubed

2 tbsp curry powder

600ml vegetable stock, homemade *(see page 16)*

100g dried split red lentils, rinsed & drained

400g chopped tomatoes

4 tbsp baby leaf spinach

2 tsp Himalayan rock salt

freshly ground black pepper

handful of coriander, finely chopped

METHOD

Heat the oil in a saucepan & gently sweat the onion & garlic for around 5 minutes to soften them.

Stir in the butternut squash & curry powder, then pour in the stock, lentils & tomatoes, & bring to the boil. Cover & simmer for around an hour, stirring occasionally, to let the squash soften & the sauce reduce.

Stir in the spinach, cover for a few minutes while it wilts, then season to taste with the salt, pepper & coriander.

Can be made in advance. Suitable for freezing, but don't add spinach until you've defrosted & reheated the curry.

Wheat Free

Gluten Free

Dairy Free

Vegetarian V

Lentil Cottage Pie

INGREDIENTS
Serves 6-8

1 tbsp extra virgin olive oil

2 large onions, finely chopped

2 cloves garlic, crushed
(10 minutes before use)

2 carrots, finely chopped

1 red pepper, finely chopped

1 tbsp corn flour, organic

1.15ltr vegetable stock, homemade *(see page 16)*

2 tsp organic yeast extract

1 tsp tamari sauce, organic
(wheat-free soy sauce)

1 tsp tomato puree
(from a glass jar)

1 bay leaf

140g brown lentils, un-cooked or cooked black eye beans

110g red lentils

900g *(approx.)* **potatoes, peeled & quartered**

55g goat's butter

4 tbsp goat's milk

½ tsp of ground pink Himalayan rock salt

a few twists of freshly ground black pepper

55g hard goat's cheese, grated

METHOD

Pre-cook the black-eye beans *(if using)*.

Sauté the onions in the olive oil, over a very low heat, for about 20 minutes, until soft & lightly caramelised, stirring to prevent sticking.

Add the garlic & all the other vegetables & cook for a further 5 minutes, stirring frequently.

Mix the corn flour with 4 tbsp. of the cold vegetable stock, until smooth.

Add the corn flour mix, stock, yeast extract, tamari sauce, tomato puree, & the bayleaf. Add the red & brown lentils.

Bring to the boil & then simmer gently for 40 minutes, adding the cooked black eye beans after 10 minutes *(if using)*.

Prepare & boil the potatoes in filtered or distilled water, until cooked through.

Pre-heat the oven to 170°C/330°F/Gas Mark 3, 10 minutes before the lentil mix has finished cooking.

Drain & mash the potatoes thoroughly, adding the goat's milk, goat's butter, pink Himalayan rock salt & the black pepper to taste.

Assemble in a large casserole dish, with the lentil mixture at the bottom, the mashed potato spread evenly over the top & finally covered with grated goat's cheese.

Bake in the oven for 20 – 25 minutes.

Ⓧ Wheat Free
Ⓢ Gluten Free
Ⓥ Vegetarian

Mediterranean Baked Squash

INGREDIENTS
Serves 6

850ml vegetable stock

200g brown rice

1.8kg butternut squash, cut in half & de-seeded

16 cherry tomatoes, quartered

125g black olives
(halved & stoned)

1 red pepper, roughly chopped

1 yellow pepper, roughly chopped

1 orange pepper, roughly chopped

2 tsp dried thyme

4 tbsp tomato puree

freshly ground black pepper

METHOD

De-seed peppers, drizzle with olive oil & roast for 45 minutes

In a large lidded pan, bring the stock to the boil & add the rice. Bring back to the boil, cover, reduce to a simmer & cook for 25 minutes until tender. Check occasionally, adding more water if boiling dry; almost all of the stock should be absorbed by the end.

Meanwhile, preheat the oven to 180°C/350°F/Gas Mark 4. Place the squash skin side down in a large ovenproof dish. Pour 150ml water in the bottom of the dish & bake for 20 minutes.

In a pan, mix together the cooked rice, tomatoes, olives, peppers, thyme & tomato puree. Season with freshly ground black pepper.

Remove the squash from the oven, spoon the rice mixture into the squash & bake for 40-50 minutes until the squash is tender. Remove from the pan & serve hot.

Wheat Free ⊗
Gluten Free ⊗
Dairy Free ⊙
Vegetarian Ⓥ

Moroccan Vegetable Tagine

INGREDIENTS
Serves 4

8 shallots

½ red peppers

1 large carrot

185g butternut squash

2.5cm piece ginger

8 dried apricots *(sulphur free)*

2 garlic cloves

400g chickpeas *(soaked & cooked)*

½ tsp ground cumin

½ tsp ground coriander

½ tsp paprika

½ tsp cinnamon

2 tbsp tomato puree

340ml vegetable stock

Himalayan rock salt

freshly ground black pepper

1 tbsp chopped pickled onion

1 tbsp chopped fresh coriander

METHOD

Set the oven temperature to 200°C/400°F/Gas Mark 6.

Peel the shallots, slice the red pepper & cut the carrot into chunks. Place these in a casserole dish.

Peel & de-seed the butternut squash & cut into bite size pieces. Cut one third into tiny dice so they will break down on cooking & form part of the sauce. Add all the butternut squash to the casserole.

Grate the ginger & press the garlic cloves & add these to the casserole along with the dried apricots & cooked chickpeas.

Mix the cumin, coriander, cinnamon & tomato puree with the stock & pour over the vegetables in the casserole dish.

Cover the casserole & cook for 50-60 minutes or until the vegetables are cooked.

Season to taste with salt & pepper. Garnish with coriander & serve with millet or baked potatoes.

Wheat Free
Gluten Free
Dairy Free
V Vegetarian

Nut Burgers

INGREDIENTS
Makes about 7

110g gluten free breadcrumbs, from homemade bread

80g hard goat's cheese, grated

1 large carrot, finely grated

1 medium onion, very finely chopped or finely grated

¼ tsp pink Himalayan rock salt

a few twists of freshly ground black pepper

1 egg, beaten *(organic)*

1 tsp organic yeast extract

2 tbsp tomato sauce, homemade

80g Brazil nuts, chopped

80g almonds, chopped

80g hazelnuts, chopped

1 tbsp extra virgin olive oil

METHOD

Put all the prepared ingredients into a large mixing bowl & mix thoroughly by hand.

Preheat the oven to 170°C/330°F/ Gas Mark 3.

Taking a handful of the mixture at a time, form them into burger shapes.

Lightly grease the baking tray & brush the nut burgers with the olive oil & bake for about 15 minutes or fry in the olive oil over a low heat until just cooked through (about 15-20 minutes), turning once.

Alternatively, make a nut loaf by pressing the mixture into a greased bread tin drizzling over with extra virgin olive oil & baking for 30 minutes at 160°C/320°F/Gas Mark 3.

To freeze: *arrange in a single layer on a plate & put into the freezer. Then transfer them into a Pyrex dish with an airtight plastic lid and return them to the freezer.*

To cook from frozen: *bake in a pre-heated oven (170°C/330°F/Gas Mark 3)for about 20 minutes, until piping hot all the way through, or gently fry from frozen for 20–25 minutes.*

Wheat Free
Gluten Free
Dairy Free
Vegetarian

VEGETABLE DISHES

Pasta With Broccoli & Pine Nuts

INGREDIENTS
Serves 4

450g broccoli

2 tbsp coconut oil or organic olive oil

1 onion, chopped

2 garlic cloves, crushed

1 passata jar tomatoes

2 tbsp pine nuts

85g sultanas

350g brown rice pasta

Himalayan rock salt *(to season)*

freshly ground black pepper
(to season)

METHOD

Divide the broccoli into florets & briefly steam in a pan of boiling water for 6-7 minutes. Drain well & keep warm.

Heat the oil in a pan & cook the onion & garlic for 5 minutes until the onion is soft but not brown.

Add the tomatoes & season with salt & pepper & simmer for a few minutes. Add the broccoli & sultanas.

Toast the pine nuts in a dry pan for a minute or two until they start to turn golden.

Cook the pasta in a large pan of boiling water according to the directions on the packet.

Drain & transfer to a serving dish. Mix with the broccoli mixture & the pine nuts.

- Wheat Free
- Gluten Free
- Dairy Free
- V Vegetarian

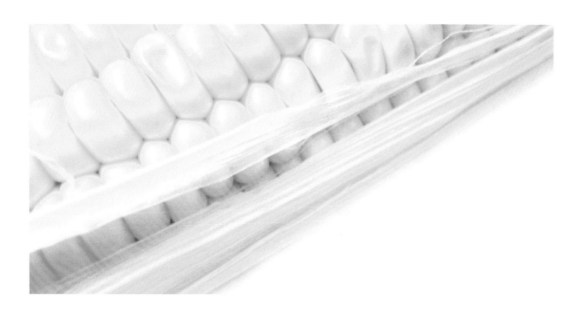

Red Kidney Bean With Sweetcorn & Tomatoes

INGREDIENTS
Serves 4

400g red kidney beans, soaked & cooked

300g sweetcorn *(off the cob)*

250g cherry tomatoes, halved

4 spring onions, chopped

a small handful of fresh coriander, chopped

Dressing:

2 tbsp coconut oil or organic olive oil

2 tbsp lemon juice *(1-2 lemons)*

Himalayan rock salt

freshly ground black pepper

METHOD

In a large bowl, combine the red kidney beans with the sweetcorn, tomatoes, spring onion, & the chopped coriander.

In a small bowl whisk together the olive oil, lemon juice & salt.

Pour the dressing over the vegetables. Serve the salad at room temperature or slightly chilled.

Wheat Free
Gluten Free
Dairy Free
Vegetarian Ⓥ

Shitake Mushroom Risotto

INGREDIENTS
Serves 4

2 tbsp coconut oil or organic olive oil

1 large onion, peeled & chopped

2 garlic cloves, peeled & finely chopped

150g pot barley, rinsed & drained

1 wheat-free vegetable stock cube

120g shitake mushrooms, trimmed & finely sliced

2 tbsp chopped fresh parsley

METHOD

Heat 1 tbsp. oil & 1 tbsp. water in a medium sized pan. Add the onion & garlic & cook over a low heat until soft but not coloured.

Stir in the barley, add 1.5ltr cold water & the stock cube. Bring to the boil, then lower the heat & allow to simmer for about 40 minutes, or until the barley is tender & all the liquid has been absorbed.

Heat the remaining oil in a small pan & sauté the mushrooms for 2-3 minutes.

Stir into the risotto mixture with the freshly chopped parsley & serve.

Wheat Free
Dairy Free
V Vegetarian

Shitake, Spring Onion & Bok Choi Stir Fry With Quinoa

INGREDIENTS
Serves 1

60g quinoa, washed

a handful of spring onions, washed & sliced

1 tbsp extra virgin olive oil

10 shitake mushrooms, washed & sliced

2 stalks bok choi, washed & sliced

1 garlic clove, chopped

1 tbsp tamari *(wheat-free)* **soy sauce**

METHOD

Bring a saucepan of water to the boil, add the quinoa & gently simmer for 15-20 minutes until cooked.

Meanwhile, in a wok, cook the spring onions in the olive oil for a couple of minutes. Add the shitake mushrooms, bok choi & garlic & continue to stir-fry for 1 minute. Toss in the tamari & stir-fry for a further couple of minutes.

Drain the cooked quinoa & serve with the stir-fry on top.

Wheat Free
Gluten Free
Dairy Free
Vegetarian V

Spicy Bean Pot

INGREDIENTS
Serves 2

400g baked beans, homemade
(see page 44)

2 shallots, chopped

2 tbsp tomato puree

1 tsp curry powder

15g sultanas

2 oat cakes

METHOD

Place the beans in a medium size saucepan with the shallots, tomato puree, curry powder & sultanas. Heat through gently & simmer for 2-3 minutes.

Divide the bean mixture between two small bowls & serve the oat cakes alongside.

Wheat Free
Dairy Free
V Vegetarian

Spicy Chickpea Patties

INGREDIENTS
Serves 4

2 tsp cumin seeds

2 tsp coriander seeds

800g chickpeas *(soaked & cooked)*

4 spring onions, chopped

1 tbsp chopped fresh red chilli

2 egg whites

1 tbsp organic olive oil

METHOD

Lightly crush the cumin & coriander seeds in a pestle & mortar (or crush using end of rolling pin & a small bowl).

Place the chickpeas in a food processor or use a hand blender & roughly blend. Add the seeds, spring onions, chilli & egg whites & pulse a couple of times until blended.

Divide the mixture into eight & shape into patties. Add the oil to a frying pan & gently cook for 4-5 minutes, turning occasionally until golden. Take care when turning them as they are quite fragile.

Wheat Free
Gluten Free
Dairy Free
Vegetarian

Spinach Cakes

INGREDIENTS
Makes 12

650g spinach, washed
(leave stems if not tough)

3 tbsp organic olive oil

1 cup pine nuts

2 cloves garlic, minced

2 organic eggs, whisked

½ cup organic raisins

1 tsp Himalayan rock salt

METHOD

Wilt the spinach, in a large covered saucepan, for 5 minutes over a low heat *(do not add water)*.

Drain & cool; gently squeeze moisture out of the spinach.

Place spinach in a food processor & pulse until coarsely blended; set to one side.

In a small skillet warm the oil add the pine nuts & sauté until golden brown.

Add garlic to skillet & sauté for a further minute.

In a large bowl combine the pine nut mixture, blended spinach, eggs, raisins and salt.

Spread mixture into a greased baking dish & bake for 30-40 minutes in a preheated oven at 180°C/350°F/Gas Mark 4.

Cut into 12 pieces & serve.

- Wheat Free
- Gluten Free
- Dairy Free
- V Vegetarian

Spinach & Pumpkin Risotto

INGREDIENTS
Serves 2

METHOD

1 onion

1 garlic clove

1 tbsp olive oil

455g pumpkin flesh

115g baby spinach leaves

1tbsp chopped fresh oregano

1 tsp grated lemon rind

140ml vegetable stock

400g cooked brown rice
(200g uncooked)

1 tbsp chopped fresh parsley

Himalayan rock salt

freshly ground black pepper

parsley to garnish

Dice the onion & press the garlic clove. Sweat these in olive oil until the onions begin to soften.

De-seed the pumpkin & cut the flesh into 2.5cm cubes. Add to the onion & continue to sweat the vegetables, stirring occasionally, until the pumpkin is just cooked, this takes a little while so don't turn up the heat & try to rush it.

Add the spinach, oregano, lemon rind & the stock. Bring to the boil & simmer until the spinach is cooked & the pumpkin is just starting to break up.

Add the rice & parsley & heat through. Season to taste with salt & pepper; serve in individual bowls, garnish with parsley.

Wheat Free
Gluten Free
Dairy Free
Vegetarian **V**

Sweet Potato Frittata

INGREDIENTS
Serves 4-6

2 sweet potatoes peeled & chopped into cubes

1ltr vegetable stock
(organic vegetable bouillon)

knob of Goat's butter

1 tsp coconut oil

1 garlic clove finely chopped

1 small red onion finely chopped

2 red peppers de-seeded & finely chopped

large handful of washed rocket
(chopped)

3 medium organic eggs

2 tbsp organic goat's milk

METHOD

Grease a 20cm round cake tin.

Boil the sweet potatoes in the vegetable stock for 10 minutes until soft, then drain & roughly mash with a fork.

In a frying pan heat the butter & oil. Add the garlic onion & pepper. When the onions are soft add the mashed sweet potatoes & rocket.

Whisk together the eggs & milk then add the potato mixture & pour into the cake tin. Bake in the oven for 15 minutes. Take it out & gently but firmly pat down the mixture to help make it solid put it back in the oven for another 15 minutes. It may well rise in the centre from time to time but don't worry, it will sink down when it cools.

Cut in wedges to serve.

VEGETABLE DISHES

Wheat Free
Gluten Free
V Vegetarian

Tofu & Bean Burgers

INGREDIENTS
Serves 6-8

1 onion, peeled & quartered

1 garlic clove, peeled & chopped

1 carrot, trimmed peeled & grated

400g red kidney beans
(soaked & cooked)

220g tofu, cut in 2cm cubes

75g sunflower seeds

1 small bunch fresh parsley

2 tsp wheat-free vegetable
bouillon powder

METHOD

Preheat the oven to 200°C/400°F/
Gas Mark 7. Line a baking tray with
greaseproof paper.

Place all the ingredients in a food
processor & blend until the mixture is
roughly chopped but not smooth.

Remove the blade, take handfuls of
the mixture & shape into medium
sized balls. Place on the baking tray
& press down gently to form burger
shapes. You should get 6-8 burgers.

Transfer to the oven & bake for
25 minutes or until golden brown
in colour.

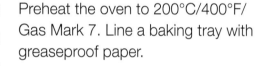

Wheat Free 🌾
Gluten Free 🌾
Dairy Free 🥛
Vegetarian Ⓥ

Vegetable Casserole

INGREDIENTS
Serves 4

225g carrots, sliced

350g turnips, diced

2 leeks, sliced

1 red onion, chopped

2 garlic cloves, crushed

150g fine green beans, halved

350g cauliflower, broken into florets

1 tsp paprika

1 tsp ground coriander

300ml vegetable stock, homemade *(see page 16)*

400g tomato passata

1 tsp dried mixed herbs

Himalayan rock salt

freshly ground black pepper

METHOD

Place the carrots, turnips, leeks, red onion, garlic, green beans & cauliflower in a large pan.

Sprinkle over the paprika & coriander, & stir the vegetables to coat them evenly in the spices. Add the stock & stir in the tomato passata. Season to taste.

Bring the pan to the boil. Reduce the heat, cover & simmer for 30 minutes until the vegetables are tender.

Remove the cover, turn up the heat & allow the mixture to bubble vigorously for 5 minutes to reduce some of the liquid.

Wheat Free
Gluten Free
Dairy Free
V Vegetarian

Vegetable Chilli

INGREDIENTS
Serves 4

1 tbsp mild olive oil (*organic*)

1 clove garlic, crushed

1 medium onion, finely chopped

1 medium carrot, finely chopped

1 red pepper, finely chopped

1 yellow pepper, finely chopped

800g tomato passata

2 tsp chilli powder

¼ tsp dried oregano

400g kidney beans, soaked & cooked

METHOD

Sauté vegetables in oil for 5 minutes.

Add remaining ingredients & simmer for approx 10 minutes (*until tender*).

Wheat Free
Gluten Free
Dairy Free
Vegetarian

Vegetable Curry

INGREDIENTS
Serves 8

Curry Sauce:

15g goat's butter

1 tbsp extra virgin olive oil

2 medium onions, chopped

6 cloves garlic, crushed

2.5cm fresh ginger, grated

2 tbsp coriander seed, ground

2 tbsp cumin, ground

2 tsp garam masala

½ tsp chilli powder

1 tsp yellow mustard powder

2 tsp turmeric

1 tsp black onion seeds *(optional)*

1 bay leaf

Himalayan rock salt *(to season)*

a few twists of freshly ground black pepper *(to season)*

1 carton coconut cream

570ml vegetable stock, homemade *(see page 16)*

Vegetables for the Curry:

80g green *(French)* beans cut into 5cm pieces

4 small potatoes, cut into halves

¼ of a cauliflower cut into small florets

1 large carrot, sliced

55g red lentils, washed

Wheat Free
Gluten Free
V Vegetarian

108

METHOD

Curry Sauce:

Gently heat the olive oil in a heavy based pan over the lowest possible heat.

Add the onion & sauté in the oil for approx 15 minutes, until sweet & starting to caramelize. Stir occasionally to prevent sticking.

Measure all the spices into a dish.

Add the garlic & ginger to the onions & continue to sauté for another couple of minutes.

Add the spices & stir for about 30 seconds, then add a couple of teaspoons of the vegetable stock & continue to stir for a few seconds to lift the spices from the base of the pan.

Add the rest of the stock, the coconut milk, bay leaf & seasoning.

Bring to simmering point & simmer for 10–15 minutes.

Leave to cool
(to develop the flavour).

Remove the bay leaf.

Blend using a hand-blender.

Divide the sauce into 2 portions.

Vegetable Curry :
(Use half the sauce to serve 4 people):

Put the prepared raw vegetables into a casserole dish

Stir in one half portion of the sauce.

Bake for 30 minutes at 160°C/315°F/ Gas Mark 3.

FISH

Fighting Back with Food

Baked Salmon

INGREDIENTS
Serves 2

2 x 170g salmon fillets

1 tbsp fresh rosemary

1 tbsp fresh basil

1 tbsp fresh parsley

2 cloves garlic, minced

1 tsp Himalayan rock salt

juice of an orange

juice of a lemon

METHOD

In a medium glass bowl, prepare marinade by mixing all ingredients. Place salmon fillets in a medium glass baking dish & cover with the marinade. Marinate in the refrigerator for about 1 hour, turning occasionally.

Preheat oven to190°C/375°F/ Gas Mark 5.

Bake salmon in marinade for 35-45 minutes, until easily flaked with a fork.

Wheat Free
Gluten Free
Dairy Free

Fish Bites

INGREDIENTS
Serves 4

1-2 tbsp extra virgin olive oil

140g gluten free homemade breadcrumbs

a pinch of pink Himalayan rock salt

a pinch of paprika

a pinch of sage

clove of garlic

a few twists of freshly ground black pepper

2 eggs, beaten

4 fillets of cod, salmon or pollock, cut into strips

3 tbsp white rice or gluten free flour, for coating the fish

METHOD

Grease a baking tray with olive oil, preferably using stoneware or an enamelled baking tray.

Make the breadcrumbs, leaving them in the blender.

Add the garlic, sage, paprika & seasoning to the breadcrumbs & blend again until thoroughly mixed.

Pre-heat the oven to 170°C/330°F/ Gas Mark 3.

One at a time, dip the fish pieces into a bowl of the flour to coat evenly, then a bowl of the beaten egg, then into the breadcrumb mix, coating them all thoroughly.

Place them on the greased baking tray.

Gently coat the top of the strip with olive oil, using a pastry brush.

Bake them in the oven, turning half way through, for 15 minutes or until golden brown.

Wheat Free
Gluten Free
Dairy Free

Grilled Salmon With Ginger, Garlic & Coriander

INGREDIENTS
Serves 2

2 salmon fillets

1 garlic clove

2.5cm piece ginger

1 tbsp chopped fresh coriander

1 tbsp organic olive oil

1 tbsp lemon juice

Himalayan rock salt *(to season)*

freshly ground black pepper *(to season)*

METHOD

Line a baking tray with foil. Dry the fish & place it on the foil.

Press the garlic clove, finely grate the ginger & combine these with the coriander & olive oil – pour over the fish. Season with salt & pepper.

Grill the fish on full power for approximately 10 minutes. The length of time required will depend upon the thickness of the fish. Baste the fish with juices while it is cooking & turn down the heat if the fish is browning too quickly.

Serve immediately with salad or cooked vegetables.

Wheat Free
Gluten Free
Dairy Free

Herb & Nut Crusted Tuna

INGREDIENTS
Serves 2

2 tbsp chopped almonds

2 tbsp chopped fresh coriander

Himalayan rock salt *(to season)*

freshly ground black pepper
(to season)

280g tuna steaks

1 tbsp organic olive oil

METHOD

Set the oven temperature to 200°C/400°F/Gas Mark 6.

Mix the chopped almonds, coriander & a sprinkle of salt & pepper on a plate.

Dry the tuna steaks on kitchen towel & brush both sides with olive oil. Dip each side of the steaks in the herb & nuts mixture.

Place the steaks on a baking tray & bake at the top of the oven, uncovered, for approximately 10 minutes. The time required will depend on the thickness of the fish. Tuna fish should be slightly pink inside when cooked.

Serve immediately with salad or vegetables.

Wheat Free
Gluten Free
Dairy Free

Salmon Fishcakes

INGREDIENTS
Serves 6-8

600g sweet potatoes, roughly chopped

2 garlic cloves crushed

6 spring onions, finely sliced

2 tbsp finely chopped flat leaf parsley

¼ tsp finely grated fresh ginger

400g salmon fillet skinned & roughly chopped

2 tsp dijon mustard

2 tbsp organic mayonnaise

organic olive oil *(for brushing)*

METHOD

Cook the potatoes in a large saucepan of boiling, distilled water for 10 minutes until tender. Drain, return to the pan & mash until smooth. Transfer to a large mixing bowl & set aside.

Place the garlic, spring onions, parsley, ginger & salmon in a food processor or blender & process until well mixed.

Add the fish to the potatoes, with the mustard & mayonnaise. Use your fingers to combine the mixture evenly.

Divide the mixture into 16 portions & form each one into a flat cake. Grease & line a baking tray. Space the fishcakes on the baking sheet, cover & chill for 30-40 minutes.

Brush the fishcakes with olive oil & bake in a preheated oven 190°C Gas Mark 5, for 15-20 minutes or until the cakes are lightly browned & cooked through.

FISH DISHES

Wheat Free
Gluten Free
Dairy Free

Sea Bass With Braised Fennel & Roast New Potatoes

INGREDIENTS
Serves 4

500g sea bass fillets

1 tbsp organic olive oil

1 lemon, sliced into wedges

freshly ground black pepper

FOR THE FENNEL:

1 tbsp organic olive oil

2 fennel bulbs, sliced, with outer leaves & stalks removed

50ml vegetable stock, homemade
(see page 16)

FOR THE POTATOES:

700g baby new potatoes

drizzle of organic olive oil

sprinkle of Himalayan rock salt

METHOD

Preheat the oven to 180°C/350°F/ Gas Mark 4.

Braised fennel; Heat the oil in a pan & sweat the fennel for around 5-8 minutes, until it starts to soften. Add the stock & braise for around 15 minutes or until very soft & translucent.

Rinse & dry the potatoes, chop any large ones in half, so they are roughly all the same size & will cook evenly. Place the potatoes in a roasting tin & drizzle with a little oil then sprinkle with salt. Shake the tin to coat the potatoes evenly & place in the oven. Cook the potatoes for about an hour, taking the tray out & shaking halfway through to turn the potatoes.

Wash the fish, pat it dry & season it with a little salt.

When the potatoes are ready, heat the oil in a large frying pan & fry the fish for 4-6 minutes, turning halfway through when the bottom is starting to look white & cooked, to make the skin crisp. Don't over-cook the fish; this will ruin the delicate texture & flavour.

Serve immediately, accompanied by the potatoes, fennel & a little of the fennel's braising liquor if there is any left over, some lemon wedges to squeeze over the top & lots of freshly ground black pepper.

⊗ Wheat Free
⊗ Gluten Free
⊗ Dairy Free

118

Steamed Salmon With Stir Fried Shitake

INGREDIENTS
Serves 2

2 salmon fillets

2 tsp organic olive oil

150g shitake mushrooms, brushed or wiped clean & thickly sliced

unlimited vegetables for stir-frying
(e.g: 200g beansprouts; a sliced red pepper; handful of baby corn; a couple of handfuls of baby or young leaf spinach; shredded spring greens)

1-2 tbsp tamari sauce
(to taste)

METHOD

Steam the salmon for 12-15 minutes, or until cooked *(the fish should flake easily when pressed).*

Meanwhile, heat the oil in a wok or frying pan *(preferably one with a lid)* & stir-fry the mushrooms for a few minutes, or until they soften & turn golden.

Add the vegetables & tamari sauce & turn down the heat to a gentle simmer. Cover the pan with a lid *(or a couple of sheets of damp kitchen paper)* to allow the vegetables to steam-fry.

Wheat Free
Gluten Free
Dairy Free

Teriyaki Salmon

INGREDIENTS
Serves 4

600g thick salmon fillet, skinned

2 tbsp organic honey

1 tsp tamari sauce

2 tbsp tomato ketchup, homemade
(see page 14)

1 tsp sesame oil

½ tsp finely grated fresh root ginger

2 tsp roasted sesame seeds

METHOD

Cut the salmon into bite-sized pieces & place them in a shallow dish in a single layer.

In a small bowl mix together the honey, tamari sauce, ketchup, sesame oil & ginger until well combined.

Pour this mixture over the salmon & toss to coat evenly. Cover & marinate for 20-30 minutes.

Place the salmon pieces in a single layer on a lightly oiled grill pan. Cook under a medium-hot grill for 6-8 minutes. Remove from the grill & sprinkle over the sesame seeds.

Wheat Free
Gluten Free
Dairy Free

CHICKEN DISHES

RECIPES 4 LIFE

Fighting Back with Food

Chicken Breasts Stuffed With Olives, Sage & Walnuts

INGREDIENTS
Serves 2

4 organic chicken breasts, skinless & boneless

150g kalamata olives, pitted

1 garlic clove

15g fresh sage leaves

100g walnut halves

4 tbsp organic olive oil

freshly ground black pepper

Can be made in advance. The chicken can be stuffed & kept in the fridge or cooked & served cold.

METHOD

Preheat the oven to 180°C/350°F/ Gas Mark 4. Rub a little oil over the base of a roasting tin.

Carefully cut a slit in the side of each chicken breast to create a pocket.

Blend, or finely chop & mix together, the olives, garlic, sage, walnuts & oil until fairly smooth.

Stuff each chicken breast with the olive mixture. Rub the excess over the top of each chicken breast & place them in the roasting tin.

Put the roasting tin on a baking tray & cook for around 20-25 minutes or until the meat juices run clear. Sprinkle with black pepper before serving.

CHICKEN DISHES

Wheat Free
Gluten Free
Dairy Free

Chicken Curry

INGREDIENTS
Serves 8

Curry Sauce:

15g goat's butter

1 tbsp extra virgin olive oil

2 medium onions, chopped

6 cloves garlic, crushed

2.5cm fresh ginger, grated

2 tbsp coriander seed, ground

2 tbsp cumin, ground

2 tsp garam masala

½ tsp chilli powder

1 tsp yellow mustard powder

2 tsp turmeric

1 tsp black onion seeds
(optional)

1 bay leaf

a pinch of pink Himalayan
rock salt

a few twists of freshly ground
black pepper

1 carton coconut cream

570ml vegetable stock,
homemade *(see page 16)*

METHOD

For Chicken Curry:
(use half the sauce, serving 4 people
with 3 chicken breast fillets)

Gently heat the olive oil in a heavy based
pan over the lowest possible heat.

Add the onion & sauté in the oil for
approx 15 minutes, until sweet &
starting to caramelize stir occasionally
to prevent sticking.

Measure all the spices into a dish.

Add the garlic & ginger to the onions
& continue to sauté for another couple
of minutes.

Add the spices & stir for about 30 seconds,
then add a couple of teaspoons of the
vegetable stock & continue to stir for a few
seconds to lift the spices from the base of
the pan.

Add the rest of the stock, the coconut milk,
bay leaf & seasoning.

Bring to simmering point & simmer for
10–15 minutes.

Leave to cool (to develop the flavour).

Remove the bay leaf & blend using
a hand-blender.

Divide the sauce into 2 portions.

Chicken Curry:

Dice the raw chicken breasts, place
in a casserole dish & stir in one portion
of the sauce.

Bake for 40 minutes at 160°C/315°F/
Gas Mark 3.

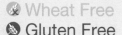
Wheat Free
Gluten Free

Chicken Satay Kebabs

INGREDIENTS
Serves 2

2 large organic chicken breasts

Marinade:

1 garlic clove

1 tsp organic olive oil

1 tsp sesame oil

1 tbsp lemon juice

1 tsp tamari sauce *(optional)*

up to ¼ tsp chilli powder

Himalayan rock salt *(to season)*

freshly ground black pepper *(to season)*

Satay Sauce:

4 tbsp cashew nut butter

140ml coconut milk

1tbsp lemon juice

1 pressed garlic clove

1 level tsp honey *(optional)*

1 tsp tamari sauce *(optional)*

METHOD

To make the Marinade:

Press the garlic clove & place in a bowl with the olive oil, sesame oil, lemon juice, tamari sauce, chilli powder & a little salt & pepper. Whisk to combine the ingredients.

Cut the chicken breasts into bite size chunks, add the marinade & set aside for a few hours but at least while you prepare the satay sauce.

To make the Satay Sauce: Place all the ingredients in a pan & heat, stirring occasionally, until well combined. Season to taste, with salt & pepper.

Thread the chicken pieces onto two large or four small skewers folding over where the chicken is thinner so the pieces are evenly sized.

Cook under a hot grill for approximately. 5 minutes each side, or until the chicken is cooked. Baste during cooking with any remaining marinade.

Wheat Free
Gluten Free
Dairy Free

Chicken & Walnut Pâté

INGREDIENTS
Serves 2

115g cooked chicken breast

85g walnuts

4 tbsp soya yoghurt

4 tbsp rice milk

1 level tsp dried tarragon or 1 tbsp chopped fresh tarragon

Himalayan rock salt

freshly ground black pepper

1 tbsp chopped walnuts *(to garnish)*

METHOD

Cut the chicken into pieces & process with walnuts, soya yoghurt, rice milk, & tarragon until combined but not smooth.

Season to taste with salt & pepper, garnish with chopped walnuts & serve.

 Wheat Free
Gluten Free
Dairy Free

Crispy Breaded Chicken Strips

INGREDIENTS
Serves 4

2 cloves garlic, crushed

1-2 tbsp olive oil, extra virgin

140g gluten free homemade breadcrumbs

1 tsp sage, dried (or 2 tsp fresh)

2 tsp paprika

a pinch of pink Himalayan rock salt

a few twists of freshly ground black pepper

2 eggs, beaten

4 chicken breasts, cut into strips

3 tbsp white rice or gluten free flour, for coating the chicken strips

METHOD

Crush the garlic & leave to rest for 10 minutes before using.

Grease a baking tray with olive oil, preferably using stoneware or an enamelled baking tray.

Make the breadcrumbs, leaving them in the blender.

Add the garlic, sage, paprika & seasoning to the breadcrumbs & blend again until thoroughly mixed.

Pre-heat the oven to 170°C/330°F/ Gas Mark 3.

One at a time, dip the chicken strips into a bowl of the flour to coat evenly, then a bowl of the beaten egg, then into the breadcrumb mix, coating them all thoroughly.

Place them on the greased baking tray.

Gently coat the top of the strip with olive oil, using a pastry brush.

Bake in the oven, turning half way through, for 25 minutes or until golden brown.

CHICKEN DISHES

Wheat Free

Gluten Free

Dairy Free

127

Moroccan Style Chicken

INGREDIENTS
Serves 4

1 tbsp coconut oil or organic olive oil

2 red onions, sliced

4 organic chicken breasts, skin & fat removed, cubed

700g butternut squash, unpeeled, seeds scraped out & cubed

1 tsp ground cinnamon

1 tsp ground ginger

1 tsp turmeric

1ltr chicken stock

fresh coriander & mint for sprinkling

freshly ground black pepper

METHOD

Heat the oil in a large saucepan & sweat the onion for 3-4 minutes, then add the chicken, squash & spices, & stir for another couple of minutes.

Pour in the stock, bring to the boil, then cover & simmer for 30 minutes. Uncover & simmer for a further 10 minutes to allow the meat to cook fully (the juices should run clear) & the sauce to thicken.

Sprinkle with coriander, mint & black pepper before serving.

 Wheat Free
Gluten Free
Dairy Free

Spanish Chicken Casserole

INGREDIENTS
Serves 4

1 tbsp organic olive oil

4 chicken breasts, chopped

1 large white onion, chopped finely

4 medium potatoes
(approx. 800g), quartered

80g roasted pine nuts

80g roasted blanched almonds

1ltr chicken stock

80ml lemon juice

4 cloves garlic, crushed

2 tbsp fresh thyme leaves

A good handful of coarsely chopped
fresh flat-leaf parsley

500g baby green beans, trimmed

2 tbsp gluten free flour

Himalayan rock salt *(to season)*

freshly ground black pepper
(to season)

METHOD

Slowly fry the onions until they are soft & set aside, then seal all the chicken pieces.

Put everything into the slow cooker *(except green beans)* & cook for 5-7 hours.

Add the green beans for the last hour.

Wheat Free
Gluten Free
Dairy Free

MEAT DISHES

RECIPES
4 LIFE

Fighting Back with Food

*Sir Ian Botham visited Alfie at
Great Ormond Street Hospital in April, 2010
along with other children receiving care.
The former England all-rounder was celebrating
the 25th anniversary of his charity walks,
which raise money & awareness for leukaemia.*

**"I have fond memories of Alfie & he
certainly was a gutsy little character.
I love this picture of us together,
Alfie in the Oakley's.**

**I am delighted to be part of this book in
memory of a special boy & knowing that the
success of this book will be Alfie's legacy
living on to help others.**

Beefy"

'Beefy' Burgers

INGREDIENTS
Makes 10

750g lean beef steak mince (organic, grass fed)

1 tbsp tomato sauce, homemade (see page 15)

1 onion, finely chopped

1 tsp ground cumin

1 tsp ground coriander seeds

1 beaten organic egg

pinch of pink Himalayan rock salt

few twists of freshly ground black pepper

115g breadcrumbs from homemade bread

METHOD

Mix all the ingredients together in a large bowl.

Take small handfuls of the mixture & shape into burgers.

TO FREEZE: *place 2 layers of grease proof paper in between each burger to prevent them sticking together & freeze in a Pyrex dish with an air-tight lid.*

TO FRY: *shallow fry them in a little extra virgin olive oil over a medium/low heat for about 20 minutes, turning regularly.*

TO OVEN COOK FRESHLY MADE BURGERS: *place the burgers in an oven proof dish & place in a pre-heated oven at 180°C/350°F/Gas Mark 4, for about 20 minutes.*

TO COOK FROM FROZEN: *place in an oven proof dish & place in a pre-heated oven at 180°C/350°F/ Gas Mark 4, for about 30 minutes, depending on thickness, until cooked right through.*

Dairy Free

Mamma's Meatballs

INGREDIENTS
Serves 4-6

1 tbsp organic olive oil

25g chopped coriander

1 onion, peeled & diced

25g chopped parsley

1 leek, trimmed & sliced

1 tbsp wholegrain mustard

2 cloves garlic, peeled & finely sliced

2 organic eggs

4 slices of homemade bread,
(see page 34)

400g brown rice

1 tsp dried oregano

½ tsp cinnamon

500g lean lamb mince

200g tomato passata

55g sunflower seeds

115g tomato puree

1 tbsp tamarai sauce

4 sprigs parsley

METHOD

Preheat oven to 190ºC/375ºF/Gas mark 5. In a wok heat the oil & stir fry the onion, leek & garlic until soft.

Whiz the bread in a food processor to makes breadcrumbs, then transfer the crumbs to a mixing bowl & mix in the oregano, mince, seeds, herbs, mustard & eggs.

Using your hands, mould the mixture into small meatballs & place on a baking tray & bake for 20-30 minutes. While the meatballs are baking add the rice to boiling water & simmer for 20 minutes.

Put the tomato passata, puree & tamarai sauce into a separate pan & stir over a low heat.

Serve the meatballs with the rice & drizzle the sauce on top.

MEAT DISHES

◔ Dairy Free

Moroccan Spiced Rice With Lamb

INGREDIENTS
Serves 4

350g organic lean lamb mince

1 onion, sliced

2 garlic cloves, crushed

½ tsp ground ginger

½ tsp ground cinnamon

1 tsp paprika

1 aubergine, diced

225g courgettes, diced

225g brown rice

400ml lamb stock

450g plum tomatoes, skinned, de-seeded & diced

2 tbsp chopped fresh mint & extra leaves to garnish

METHOD

Heat a heavy based frying pan & add the lamb mince. Dry fry for 5 minutes, draining off any excess fat.

Add the onion, garlic, ginger, cinnamon & paprika & stir well.

Add the aubergine, courgettes, rice & stock & bring to the boil. Cover & simmer for 20 minutes until the stock has been absorbed & the rice is tender.

Add the tomatoes & mint & heat through. Spoon the mixture into a warmed serving dish & scatter with a few extra mint leaves.

Wheat Free
Gluten Free
Dairy Free

CAKES, BISCUITS & DESSERTS

RECIPES 4 LIFE

Fighting Back with Food

Avocado Dessert Lollies

INGREDIENTS
Makes 4

8 medjool dates, pitted

½ cup of distilled water

3 medium avocados, pitted

1 cup coconut milk

¼ cup locally produced honey

5-7 tbsp cacao/cocoa powder

2 tsp vanilla essence

pinch of Himalayan rock salt

METHOD

Place the dates into your blender & cover with water, pack the dates down if needed, so they are covered, for most part in water. Let soak for 30 minutes.

Add in the remaining ingredients & blend until very smooth & creamy. Depending on the blender, you may need to add a little extra coconut milk or water.

Pour into small bowls & serve as pudding or pour into lolly moulds & freeze for at least 6 hours. Run under hot water to release.

You can buy 'Happy Mummy' ice cream moulds which are BPA free.

Wheat Free 🚫
Gluten Free 🚫
Dairy Free 🚫
Vegetarian Ⓥ

Banana & Berry Ice

INGREDIENTS
Serves 1

1 banana, frozen in slices

1 handful frozen berries
(e.g. raspberries, blackcurrants, blueberries, etc)

METHOD

Simply feed the fruit pieces through the juicer or blend in a food processor, blending again with a hand blender if necessary to obtain a smooth consistency.

Serve immediately.

Try Making a MANGO ICE:
½ a large (per person) ripe mango frozen in small pieces then blended.

⊗ Wheat Free
⊗ Gluten Free
⊗ Dairy Free
Ⓥ Vegetarian

Banana Cakes

INGREDIENTS
Makes 10

100g xylitol

6 tbsp organic olive oil

1 tsp vanilla extract

½ ripe banana

150g gluten free self raising flour

4 tbsp water

METHOD

Beat together Xylitol, oil & vanilla extract.

Peel & mash half a banana & beat it into the mixture.

Add the flour & water; mix well.

Spoon into cupcake cases & bake for 20 to 25 minutes in a preheated oven at 190ºC/375ºF/Gas Mark 5, until golden & just firm to the touch.

Wheat Free
Gluten Free
Dairy Free
Vegetarian V

Banana & Cinnamon Blinis

INGREDIENTS
Serves 4-6

90ml rice or coconut milk

30g goat's butter

1 banana

1 medium organic egg

55g buckwheat flour

½ tsp cinnamon

METHOD

Warm the milk & 15g of butter until the butter is just melted.

Slice the banana into thin slices.

Separate the egg & whisk the egg white until stiff.

Process & beat together the milk & butter, flour, egg yolk, & cinnamon until well mixed, then fold into the egg white using a metal spoon.

Melt a knob of the remaining butter in a 20cm/8in frying pan & pour four separate tablespoons of batter to form four little crepes. Immediately place three slices of banana in each.

Cook the blinis until golden brown, then turn over & cook on the second side. Keep warm while you repeat the process with the remaining batter.

Serve warm just as they are or add honey.

Wheat Free
Gluten Free
V Vegetarian

Beetroot Brownies

INGREDIENTS
Makes 12

250g dark chocolate, chopped

200g coconut oil

250g beetroot, cooked

3 organic eggs

a drop of vanilla extract

200g xylitol

50g cocoa powder

50g rice/coconut milk

1 tsp gluten-free baking powder

100g ground almonds

It is very important not to overcook the brownies; a skewer inserted into the centre should come out slightly sticky.

Leave to cool in the tin & then cut into squares. Put into the fridge for several hours for a wonderfully fudgy effect.

METHOD

Put the chocolate & coconut oil in a large bowl & place it over a pan of simmering water. Leave to melt, & then remove from heat.

Puree the cooked beetroot in a food processor. Add the eggs one at a time, followed by the vanilla & a little milk mix until smooth.

Sift the cocoa powder & baking powder into a bowl, add the rice/coconut milk & stir in the ground almonds. Stir the beetroot mixture into the melted chocolate & then add the dry ingredients.

Line a rectangular tin with baking paper, roughly 28 x 18cm. Pour in the mixture & place in a preheated oven at 180°C/350°F/Gas Mark 4. Bake for 25-30 minutes, until just firm to the touch.

Wheat Free 🌾
Dairy Free 🥛
Vegetarian Ⓥ

Biscotti With Pistachio & Citrus

INGREDIENTS
Makes 16

185g rice flour plus a little extra for rolling

75g xylitol

½tsp gluten free baking powder

1 large free-range or organic egg, beaten

finely grated zest of 1 orange

75g mixed dried fruit

75g unsalted pistachios, shelled, preferably with their skins on

2 drops of almond extract

✳ *Can be made in advance; Suitable for freezing.*

METHOD

Preheat the oven to 180°C/350°F/ Gas Mark 4. Line a baking tray with baking paper.

Mix the flour, xylitol & baking powder together in a mixing bowl. Stir in half of the egg & mix, then slowly mix in the remaining egg to create large breadcrumbs.

Stir in the orange zest, dried fruit & nuts, & bring the mixture together into a ball, using your hands, making sure that the fruit & nuts are evenly distributed. Taste & add a couple of drops of almond extract if you wish.

Roll the dough out on a lightly floured board & shape into a long, even sausage, around 20cm (8in) long. Flatten slightly to create the characteristic squashed shape of biscotti, then place on the baking tray & bake for around 25 minutes until golden. Remove from the oven & leave to cool for at least 15 minutes (you will need the oven again) before cutting into 16 slices.

Lay the slices out on the baking tray & return to the oven for 10 minutes, then turn the slices over & cook for a further 10 minutes, to harden and turn them golden. Cool on a wire rack before storing in an airtight container for up to 1 week.

Ⓧ Wheat Free
Ⓢ Gluten Free
Ⓓ Dairy Free
Ⓥ Vegetarian

Blueberry Pancakes

INGREDIENTS
Makes 6-8

For the blueberry compote:

300g blueberries

1 tbsp xylitol

For the Pancakes:

175g whole oat flakes, finely blended to form a flour
(using a food processor)

75g xylitol

1 large organic egg, lightly beaten

250ml unsweetened non-dairy milk
(such as rice, oat or coconut milk)

**a little coconut oil
or organic olive oil** *(for frying)*

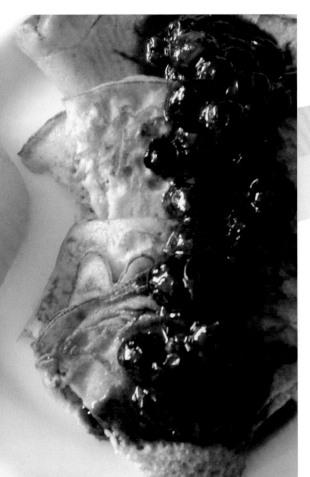

METHOD

Place the blueberries in a saucepan with a splash of water & leave to simmer gently (5 to 10 minutes) until they soften. Sweeten them to taste with the xylitol and set them to one side while you make the pancakes.

Mix the oat flour & the 75g of xylitol in a bowl.

Whisk the milk into the egg to form a batter the consistency of whipping cream, then stir into the dried ingredients. If the mixture is not particularly smooth it may be that your blender isn't powerful enough to grind the oats to a fine flour. If this is the case, blend the mixture using a hand blender to make it as smooth as possible.

Heat a couple of tablespoons of oil in the base of a large frying pan & place tablespoons of the pancake mixture in the pan (without touching each other). Fry for a minute or so on each side, or until firm & golden brown. Do this in batches so as not to crowd the pan.

Place the cooked pancakes on a plate & cover with a clean towel to keep them warm while you finish the batch.

Serve the pancakes covered with the blueberry compote.

Wheat Free 🌾
Dairy Free 🥛
Vegetarian Ⓥ

Buckwheat Pancakes

INGREDIENTS
Makes 4-6 Pancakes

100g buckwheat flour

pinch himalayan rock salt

1 organic egg

300ml rice milk or coconut milk

50g goat's butter *(melted)*

METHOD

Place flour & salt in a mixing bowl, add the egg.

Add the milk a little at a time, beat into a batter.

Mix well then leave to rest for at least an hour.

Stir the melted butter into the batter.

Lightly oil a heavy-based frying pan & heat well.

Put a good tablespoon of batter into the hot pan, rolling it around to cover the pan surface. Sprinkle with cinnamon.

Cook until golden then turn over & cook on the other side.

 Wheat Free

Gluten Free

V Vegetarian

Chocolate Cakes

INGREDIENTS
Makes 12 Muffin size cakes

110g white spelt flour

110g plain wholemeal flour

28g cocoa powder

¼ tsp bicarbonate of soda
(aluminium free)

½ tsp cream of tartar

4 organic eggs

1 tsp vanilla extract
(don't use vanilla essence)

110g rapadura sugar

2 tbsp maple syrup

110g goat's butter

5 tbsp extra virgin olive oil

3 tbsp goat's milk,
rice milk or oat milk

METHOD

Pre-heat the oven to 160°C/315°F/
Gas Mark 3.

Sieve the flours, cocoa powder,
bicarbonate of soda & cream of
tartar into a large bowl.

Add all of the other ingredients
except the goat's milk.

Beat thoroughly using
an electric mixer.

Add the goat's milk & beat again.

Either line your muffin tray with
un-bleached paper cases or grease
a stoneware muffin tray with olive oil.

Put 1 heaped tablespoon of cake
mixture into each paper case.

Bake for 15–20 minutes.

Cool on a wire rack & store in an
air-tight tin for up to 5 days

*Suitable for freezing;
Defrost overnight in the fridge.
165g xylitol & 1 tbsp of
vegetable glycerine can be used
to replace the sugar & maple
syrup when following an
anti-Candida diet.*

Vegetarian Ⓥ

Chocolate Hazelnut Brownies

INGREDIENTS
Makes 12

100g organic dark chocolate
(70% cocoa solids) **for melting**

50g organic dark chocolate
(70% cocoa solids for flavour)
finely chopped into chips

150g coconut oil

100g xylitol

2 ripe bananas, mashed

4 large organic eggs, beaten

2 tsp vanilla extract
(not artificial vanilla flavouring)

150g ground almonds

2 tsp gluten free baking powder

25g cocoa powder

200g hazelnuts, chopped

Can be made in advance.
Suitable for freezing.

METHOD

Preheat the oven to 180°C/350°F/ Gas Mark 4. Line a 22cm square baking tin with baking paper.

Melt the 100g of chocolate in a heat-proof bowl, above a pan of hot water.

Beat the coconut oil & xylitol together, then either blend in the rest of the ingredients in a food processor or, to do it by hand: beat in the chocolate, bananas, beaten eggs & vanilla extract & then stir in the chocolate chips, ground almonds, baking powder, cocoa powder & chopped hazelnuts.

Pour the mixture into the prepared tin & bake for around 20 minutes or until the mixture no longer wobbles when shaken & the top is just firm to the touch. You don't want to cook it for too long or the brownies will lose their squidgy quality. Leave to cool then cut into slices for serving.

Wheat Free
Gluten Free
Dairy Free
V Vegetarian

Cinnamon Millet Porridge

INGREDIENTS
Serves 2

250g millet

1 cinnamon stick

zest of half a lemon

2 tbsp shelled hemp seeds

METHOD

Place the millet, cinnamon & lemon zest, together with 1.25ltr of distilled water in a medium sized pan & bring to the boil. Lower the heat & simmer for 1 hour.

Serve warm with the hemp seeds sprinkled on top.

Wheat Free
Dairy Free
Vegetarian

Coconut Oat Biscuits

INGREDIENTS
Makes 10

75g coconut oil

25g xylitol

1 tbsp honey

100g whole rolled oats

50g desiccated coconut

1-2 tsp ground ginger *(optional)*

Can be made in advance.
Suitable for freezing.

METHOD

Preheat the oven to 170°C/325°F/ Gas Mark 3. Line a baking tray with paper.

Gently melt the oil & xylitol with the honey, taking care not to let it boil. Stir in the oats, coconut & ginger.

Shape the mixture into ten walnut-sized balls. The mixture will be very crumbly at this stage, so press it together firmly then place the biscuits on the baking tray.

Bake for around 20 minutes or until they're just turning golden on top. Leave to harden & cool on a wire rack.

Wheat Free
Dairy Free
V Vegetarian

CAKES, BISCUITS & DESSERTS

Country Apple Cake

INGREDIENTS
Makes 1 large Cake or 12 Cupcakes

115g organic chopped dried dates

90ml distilled water

170g organic eating apples

115g organic goat's butter

2 medium organic eggs

170g organic gluten free flour

2 rounded tsp mixed spice

2 rounded tsp gluten-free baking powder

115g organic sultanas

These make great lunch box deserts by making small muffins using bleach free cup cases.

METHOD

Grease & line a 15-18cm, deep sided cake tin. Pre-heat the oven temperature to 170°C/325°F/ Gas Mark 3.

Place the dates & water into a pan & simmer over a low heat until the water has been absorbed & the dates are soft. Allow them to cool a little.

Peel & core the apples & cut the flesh into small pieces.

Process the dates & butter until they are creamy.

Add the spice, apples & sultanas & process until everything is combined.

Fold in the flour & mix.

The mixture should be a soft dropping consistency. If it is a bit stiff add a little water until it is the desired consistency.

Place the mixture in to the cake tin & bake for 40-50 minutes or until golden brown & firm to touch.

Allow 5 minutes for the cake to cool in the tin & then turn it out onto a wire cooling rack, peeling off the lining paper.

Wheat Free ✖

Gluten Free ✖

Vegetarian ⓥ

Cranberry Almond Loaf

INGREDIENTS
Makes 1 Loaf

¾ **cup almond butter**
(at room temperature)

2 **tbsp organic olive oil**

3 **large organic eggs**

¼ **cup arrowroot powder**

1 **tsp Himalayan rock salt**

¼ **tsp gluten free baking powder**

¼ **cup dried apricots, chopped**

½ **cup cranberries**

¼ **cup sesame seeds**

¼ **cup sunflower seeds**

¼ **cup pumpkin seeds**

¼ **cup sliced almonds & 2 tbsp to sprinkle on top**

organic olive oil *(for greasing)*

rice flour *(for dusting)*

METHOD

Preheat the oven to 180°C/350°F/ Gas Mark 4 & grease a loaf pan & dust with rice flour.

In a large bowl, blend butter, olive oil & eggs with a handheld mixer until smooth & creamy.

Mix arrowroot powder, salt & baking powder; add this mixture to the creamed ingredients until thoroughly combined.

Fold in the apricots, cranberries, seeds & sliced almonds.

Pour the batter into the prepared loaf pan; sprinkle the remaining sliced almonds on top.

Bake for 40 to 50 minutes until a knife inserted into the centre comes out 'clean'.

Let cool in the pan for 1 hour, serve.

 Wheat Free
◉ Gluten Free
◉ Dairy Free
Ⓥ Vegetarian

Crunchy Muesli

INGREDIENTS
Serves 4

30g flaxseeds

2tbsp maple syrup

60g mixed nuts, chopped

30g pumpkin seeds, chopped

100g rolled oats

30g sunflower seeds, chopped

2 tbsp walnut oil

METHOD

Preheat the oven to 180°C/350°F/ Gas Mark 4.

Place all the ingredients into a mixing bowl & combine well.

Turn out into a shallow baking tin & bake in the oven for about 20 minutes until golden brown & well toasted. You will need to stir the muesli once or twice whilst cooking.

Leave to cool & store in an airtight container.

Serve with rice milk; oat milk; soya milk or yoghurt & topped with some chopped banana & berries.

Keeps for 2 weeks in an airtight container & can be doubled or tripled easily.

Wheat Free
Dairy Free
Vegetarian

Custard

METHOD

Serves 4

2 egg yolks

1 tsp vanilla extract
(don't use essence)

1 tbsp maple syrup or honey, to taste

1 tbsp corn flour *(organic)*

340ml goat's milk

Separate your egg yolks & put them in a small jug or bowl.

Add the vanilla extract, maple syrup (or honey), corn flour & 2 tbsp of the goat's milk.

Mix to a smooth paste.

Gently heat the rest of the milk in a saucepan, almost to boiling point.

Pour some of the heated milk into your egg mixture, stir rapidly, then pour it all directly back into the saucepan.

Stir the custard continuously using a wooden spoon, heating gently until the custard has thickened.

Wheat Free
V Vegetarian

Easy Fruit Cake

INGREDIENTS
Makes 1 Cake

350g mixed dried fruit

100g xylitol

100g goat's butter

150ml distilled water

1 organic egg

225g rice flour

METHOD

Heat Oven to 150°C/300°F/Gas Mark 2. Grease an 18cm cake tin.

Place fruit, xylitol, butter & water in a pan. Simmer slowly with the lid on for 20 minutes.

Allow to cool then add the beaten egg & stir in the flour.

Pour into prepared tin & bake for 1½ hours.

Wheat Free
Gluten Free
Vegetarian

Flap Jacks

INGREDIENTS
Makes 12

165g goat's butter

110g rapadura sugar

3 tbsp maple syrup

310g organic porridge oats

1 tsp ground cinnamon

METHOD

Pre-heat the oven to 160°C/315°F/ Gas Mark 3.

Gently melt the butter in a saucepan.

Add the sugar & the maple syrup, stirring to dissolve.

Add the porridge oats & cinnamon.

Stir to combine all of the ingredients.

Remove from the heat.

Line an oven-proof dish with un-bleached greaseproof paper.

Grease with extra virgin olive oil or goat's butter.

Put the mixture into the prepared dish & press down firmly using the back of a spoon.

Bake for 15–20 minutes.

Leave to cool in the dish, cutting the flapjacks to the required sizes after about 5 minutes, (while still warm).

When they have cooled completely, they can be stored in an air-tight tin for about 5 days.

Wheat Free

V Vegetarian

Gingerbread Men

INGREDIENTS
Makes 12

110g white spelt flour

110g whole meal plain flour

110g goat's butter
(at room temperature)

1 egg, beaten

4 tsp ground ginger

110 g rapadura sugar

1–2 tbsp maple syrup
(or 1 heaped tbsp of blackstrap molasses)

METHOD

Sift the flour, ground ginger & rapadura sugar into a mixing bowl.

Add the soft goat's butter & blend/mix.

In a separate bowl; beat the egg, add the maple syrup or molasses to it & beat again.

Add the egg mixture to the flour mixture.

Blend until it forms into dough. You may need to add extra flour if it is too sticky.

Turn the dough out onto a floured surface & roll out to approx ½ cm thickness, moving the dough around & re-flouring if necessary to ensure it doesn't stick.

Pre-heat the oven to 160ºC/315ºF/ Gas Mark 3.

Cut out your gingerbread men (or biscuits) & put them onto a greased baking tray.

Bake in the oven for approx 9–10 minutes, until golden.

Leave to cool slightly on the tin for a few minutes & then cool on a wire cooling rack. Store them in an air-tight tin for up to 5 days.

Vegetarian Ⓥ

Guava Smoothie

INGREDIENTS
Serves 1

1 banana, peeled

115ml fresh apple juice

1 guava, peeled

150ml goat's yoghurt (optional)

METHOD

Liquidize the ingredients together in a blender & serve.

Wheat Free
Gluten Free
V Vegetarian

Ice Lollies

INGREDIENTS

1 pint orange juice, freshly squeezed

juice of ½ a lemon

1 dsp maple syrup or honey
(or 2-3 tsp 'xylitol' dissolved in 1 tbsp of boiling water & cooled)

METHOD

Juice the oranges into a large measuring jug.

Add the other ingredients & blend, using a hand blender.

Pour into ice-lolly moulds & freeze for at least 4 hours.

When ready to eat, place the ice-lolly mould briefly under warm running water to remove the lollipop from the mould.

OTHER VARIETIES

Try adding 1 chopped fresh, ripe Mango to the recipe, using only ½ pint of juice & blend.

Fresh Berries can also be blended in with the mixture and then passed through a mouli or sieve to remove the seeds.

Try substituting fresh Apple Juice for the orange juice & add half a punnet of fresh Strawberries. Pass through a mouli or sieve to remove the seeds.

Wheat Free
Gluten Free
Dairy Free
Vegetarian V

Oatbran & Berries Smoothie

INGREDIENTS
Serves 1

1 ripe banana

115g strawberries

225ml oat milk; rice milk
or coconut milk

a handful of ice cubes

1 tbsp oat bran

1 tbsp porridge oats

1 tbsp flaxseed oil

METHOD

Liquidize the ingredients together
in a blender & serve.

⊛ Wheat Free
🍥 Dairy Free
Ⓥ Vegetarian

Orange Chocolate Coconut Clusters

INGREDIENTS
Makes 12

2 cups dark chocolate chips, 73% cacao

1 tsp orange extract

1 cup almonds, toasted & chopped

1 cup coconut, shredded & toasted

METHOD

In a medium size saucepan, melt the chocolate over low heat.

Stir in the orange extract.

Allow the toasted nuts & coconut to cool before stirring into the melted chocolate.

Make the clusters by heaping tablespoonfuls onto a parchment lined baking sheet.

Allow to cool.

If your kitchen is too warm for the clusters to set, transfer them to a plate & cool in the freezer.

Wheat Free
Gluten Free
Dairy Free
Vegetarian

"Whilst neither I, nor my family have ever been affected by the terrible illness that Alfie suffered from, I am no stranger to other types of cancer that have struck my close family & friends, so I do have some idea of the terrible impact & suffering that it has both on the patients themselves & upon their families, & there is nothing worse than when a child is affected.

Whilst I could never repay those who helped to restore the health of my loved ones, I can do something to show my gratitude & respect, by helping others in raising awareness & money for research, in the hope that one day, we will find a cure for all types of cancer."

Craig Wilson

Chef Proprietor
'Eat on the Green' Restaurant
Udny Green, Aberdeenshire, Scotland
www.eatonthegreen.co.uk

Scottish Oat Shorties With Honey

INGREDIENTS

310g gluten free flour
(& 30g extra to roll/dust pastry)

140g goat butter, softened

140g scottish porridge oats

140g warmed honey

zest of 1 lemon

5 sprigs of thyme
(remove leaves from twigs)

**140g gluten free, dairy free, egg free
chocolate to drizzle over** *(optional)*

METHOD

Pre-heat oven to 180°C/350°F/
Gas Mark 4.

Add all the ingredients together & mix to a smooth dough. Cut into small bars 6cm long & 1cm thick or use a small pastry cutter if preferred. Place the biscuits onto greaseproof paper & bake for 12 minutes.

Take out of oven & leave to cool. If desired, break up the chocolate into a heat proof bowl & then place the bowl on top of a pan with simmering, distilled water. Stir the chocolate until it has fully melted. Using a teaspoon, drizzle the chocolate over the biscuits & leave to set.

"I decided to adapt a traditional Scottish shortbread recipe, which is popular the world over, in the hope that this would bring a smile to children's faces. This biscuit is both easy to eat, almost melt-in-the-mouth, & full of flavour. The honey gives it just the right amount of sweetness & the lemon & thyme provide a blast of freshness to the palate. Honey is renowned worldwide for its healing properties & a honey local to your area will provide the most benefits for your child."

Wheat Free 🌾
Vegetarian Ⓥ

Sesame Biscuits

INGREDIENTS
Makes 16

50g goat's butter

100g rice flour

25g fine oatmeal

25g sesame seeds

25g sunflower seeds

2-3 tbsp rice or oat milk

METHOD

Pre-heat the oven to 190°C/375°F/ Gas Mark 5 & line a baking tray with a baking parchment.

Rub the butter into the flour & oatmeal & stir in the seeds. Then use the milk to bind the mixture. Use 2 tablespoons to start with, adding more milk as necessary until the mixture forms a moist ball.

Place on a floured board & roll out to about 0.3cm thick. *(If you roll the mixture too thinly it will be impossible to cut into shapes)*

Use a fluted cutter to make 5-6cm rounds & place on the prepared tray.

Place in the oven & bake for 15 minutes. Cool on wire rack.

⊗ Wheat Free
Ⓥ Vegetarian

Strawberry & Banana Cheesecake

INGREDIENTS
Serves 8-10

For the base:

100g oat cakes, *(roughly broken up)*

100g unsalted nuts & or seeds *(hazelnuts, almonds, walnuts, brazil nuts & sunflower seeds)*

50g coconut oil or 75g goat's butter

30g xylitol

1 heaped tbsp ground ginger

For the filling:

375g plain cottage cheese *(organic)*

300g natural goat's yoghurt

3 tbsp tahini

75g xylitol

1 tsp vanilla extract *(not artificial vanilla essence)*

3 medium ripe bananas

3 good handfuls of strawberries, chopped

METHOD

Preheat the oven to 160°C/325°F/ Gas Mark 3. Line a 20cm loose-bottomed cake tin with baking paper & grease the sides.

Place the oat cakes, nuts, seeds, oil or butter, xylitol & ginger in a food processor & whiz until they are the consistency of coarse breadcrumbs. Press firmly into the bottom of the lined cake tin using a metal tablespoon, so that the base is evenly covered. Bake for 10 minutes then turn off the oven & leave the base to cool in the oven with the door ajar.

Blend the cottage cheese until really smooth, add the rest of the filling ingredients & blend again until smooth (avoid any having lumps of cottage cheese remaining). Taste & add a little more xylitol to sweeten if necessary.

Pour into the cake tin & cook for around an hour or until the top is just firm to the touch. Allow to cool on a wire rack then scatter the chopped strawberries on top & chill. If you wish, puree some strawberries & drizzle over the top of the cheesecake.

Wheat Free
Vegetarian Ⓥ

Sunflower Seed & Carrot Muffins

INGREDIENTS
Makes 12

150g brown rice flour

75g fine oatmeal

1 level tsp gluten free baking powder

½ tsp ground cinnamon

¼ tsp Himalayan rock salt

2 large eggs

175ml rice milk or oat milk

2 tbsp cold-pressed mixed seed oil

100g carrots, coarsely grated

75g raisins

50g sunflower seeds

METHOD

Pre-heat the oven to 190°C/375°F/ Gas Mark 5 & grease a bun or muffin tray.

Mix the flour & oatmeal with the baking powder, cinnamon & salt.

Beat the eggs with the milk & oil.

Stir the carrots, raisins & sunflower seeds into the dry ingredients & add the egg mixture. Fold in well & spoon into the prepared bun or muffin tin.

Bake the muffins for 25 minutes, then turn out onto a wire rack.

Wheat Free
Dairy Free
V Vegetarian

Tasty Quinoa Porridge

INGREDIENTS
Serves 2

250g quinoa grains

quarter of a cinnamon stick

125ml freshly pressed apple juice

METHOD

Place the quinoa, cinnamon, apple juice & 325ml filtered water in a medium sized saucepan. Bring to the boil, then lower the heat & simmer for 7-10 minutes, or until grains are translucent.

Turn off the heat & allow to 'stand' for 15 minutes before serving.

Wheat Free
Gluten Free
Dairy Free
Vegetarian

Party Table

As a parent & a nutritional therapist I am so frequently faced with the need for preparing fun, enjoyable children's food for an occasion. I was adamant to be able to provide a children's party full of nutritious finger food suitable for all.

It is important for children to be able to
participate in fun activities that involve
food without compromising their health.
By preparing a party full of nutritious food,
all children & adults alike can tuck in.
Setting a good example to our peers may
also spread the word that nutrition most
certainly does not come at the cost of
flavour, variety and fun.

Jo Gamble BA (hons) Dip CNM MFNTP MBANT

RECIPES 4 LIFE

Writing a recipe book like this one is far from a solitary experience.
We have many people to thank for their participation,
kind words of encouragement & support however, without the following,
the creation of this book would not have been possible:

Sir Ian Botham, *for his addition to the book*

Arlene Danton, *Designer & Creator of the book*

Gail Gamble, *collaborator of the original recipes*

Roger Phillips & Students *from the Catering & Hospitality
Department of* **Thanet Technical College,** *Broadstairs,
for their creation of the dishes & Food Photography*

Gary Rhodes, *for his addition to the book*

Jackie White, *for donating various
recipes to the book*

Craig Wilson, *for his addition to the book*

Fighting Back with Food